HANUMAN CHALISA

my HANUMAN CHALISA

DEVDUTT PATTANAIK

Illustrations by the author

RUPA

Published by
Rupa Publications India Pvt. Ltd 2017
7/16, Ansari Road, Daryaganj
New Delhi 110002

Sales Centres:

Allahabad Bengaluru Chennai
Hyderabad Jaipur Kathmandu
Kolkata Mumbai

Cover illustration: Hanuman carrying the mountain bearing the Sanjivani herb while crushing the demon Kalanemi underfoot.

ISBN: 978-81-291-4795-0

First impression 2017

10 9 8 7 6 5 4 3 2 1

Design and typeset in Garamond by Special Effects, Mumbai
Printed by Thomson Press India Ltd., Faridabad

To the trolls, without and within

Contents

Why *My Hanuman Chalisa?*

One of the things that catch your eye in the middle of a horrifyingly crowded Mumbai local train is the sight of people sitting or standing in a corner, reading from a tiny chapbook sold in roadside shops near temples. Most popular of these chapbooks is the Hanuman Chalisa. In the midst of the crushing inhumanity that is urban life, you see a glow on the reader's face. It is the most powerful expression of personal Hinduism that one can encounter on India's streets.

I have always wondered what the Hanuman Chalisa is and what is in it that makes it so popular. Its language—Awadhi—is an old dialect of Hindi, one of the many languages of India. Do people reading it understand what they are reading? Or does the gentle poetic rhythm calm the nervous heart, as it prepares to face the day? Or is it simply a ritual exercise, where the point is to do, not think or feel?

So I decided to explore this popular religious work through which a Hindu god is made accessible to the masses. I realized that reading this chapbook is completely voluntary, as in all things Hindu. It is neither a commandment of a guru, nor a prescription of a priest. Its popularity is organic. Its ordinariness makes it sublime.

As I explored this work, I realized each line allows us to leap into the vast body of Hindu thought, a heritage of over 4,000 years ago, much as Hanuman leapt from his cradle to the sun, or across the sea towards Lanka, or over land towards the mountain bearing the Sanjivani herb, always returning to find Ram. From the particular, we traverse the universal, and finally return to the personal.

As you go through the forty-three verses in this book, you will notice how sensitively the poet has structured his work, how it creates a temple in the mind, and enshrines a deity in that temple, and how the verses take us from ideas of birth, through ideas of adventure, duty and glory, to the ideas of death and rebirth.

In my work, I have always avoided the academic approach, as scholars are too busy seeking 'the' truth while I am interested in expanding 'my' truth and the truth of my readers. If you seek 100% perfection, you often lose 99% of readers in cantankerous and often self-serving debates; but if you seek 90% perfection, you are able to reach out to over 90% of readers through thought-provoking elaborations that seek not to convince but to enrich. And that is good enough for me. Hence I present to you my Hanuman Chalisa, firmly anchored in the belief that:

Within infinite myths lies an eternal truth
Who sees it all?
Varuna has but a thousand eyes
Indra, a hundred
You and I, only two.

The Text

The Text

Shri guru charan saroj-raj nija manu mukura sudhaari.
Baranau Raghubara Vimala Jasu jo dayaka phala chari.

Buddhi-heen tanu janikay sumirow pavanakumara.
bala-buddhi vidya dehoo mohee harahu klesa vikaara.

1. *Jai Hanuman gyan gun sagar. Jai Kapish tihun lok ujagar.*
2. *Ram doot atulit bala dhama. Anjani-putra Pavan-sut nama.*
3. *Mahabir Bikram Bajrangi. Kumati nivar sumati ke sangi.*
4. *Kanchan varan viraj subesa. Kanan kundal kunchit kesa.*
5. *Hath vajra aur dhvaja biraje. Kaandhe moonj janehu sajai.*
6. *Sankar-suvan Kesari nandan. Tej prataap maha jag bandan.*
7. *Vidyavaan guni ati chatur. Ram kaj karibe ko aatur.*
8. *Prabhu charitra sunibe ko rasiya. Ram Lakhan Sita man basiya.*
9. *Sukshma roop dhari Siyahi dikhava. Vikat roop dhari Lank jarava.*
10. *Bhima roop dhari asur sanghare. Ramachandra ke kaj sanvare.*
11. *Laye Sanjivan Lakhan jiyaye. Shri Raghuvir harashi ur laye.*
12. *Raghupati kinhi bahut badai. Tum mam priye Bharat hi sam bhai.*
13. *Sahas badan tumharo jasa gaave. Asa kahi Shripati kanth lagaave.*
14. *Sankadhik Brahmaadi muneesa. Narad-Sarad sahita Aheesa.*
15. *Jam Kubera Digpaal jahan te. Kavi kovid kahi sake kahan te.*
16. *Tum upkar Sugrivahin keenha. Ram milaye rajpad deenha.*
17. *Tumharo mantra Vibhishan maana. Lankeshwar bhaye sub jag jana.*
18. *Yug sahastra jojan par Bhanu. Leelyo tahi madhur phal janu.*
19. *Prabhu mudrika meli mukh mahee. Jaladhi langhi gaye achraj nahee.*

20. *Durgam kaj jagath ke jete. Sugam anugraha tumhre tete.*

21. *Ram dwaare tum rakhvare. Hoat na agya bin paisare.*

22. *Sub sukh lahae tumhari sarna. Tum rakshak kahu ko darna.*

23. *Aapan tej samharo aapai. Teenhon lok hank te kanpai.*

24. *Bhoot pisaach nikat nahin aavai. Mahabir jab naam sunavae.*

25. *Nase rog harae sab peera. Japat nirantar Hanumat Beera.*

26. *Sankat se Hanuman chudavae. Man, kram, vachan dhyan jo lavai.*

27. *Sab par Ram tapasvee raja. Tin ke kaj sakal tum saja.*

28. *Aur manorath jo koi lavai. Sohi amit jeevan phal pavai.*

29. *Chaaron jug partap tumhara. Hai persidh jagat ujiyara.*

30. *Sadhu sant ke tum rakhware. Asur nikandan Ram dulhare.*

31. *Ashta-sidhi nav nidhi ke dhata. As bar deen Janki mata.*

32. *Ram rasayan tumhare pasa. Sada raho Raghupati ke dasa.*

33. *Tumhare bhajan Ram ko pavai. Janam-janam ke dukh bisraavai.*

34. *Ant-kaal Raghuvir-pur jayee. Jahan janam Hari-bhakt kahayee.*

35. *Aur devta chit na dharehi. Hanumat se hi sarve sukh karehi.*

36. *Sankat kate mite sab peera. Jo sumirai Hanumat Balbeera.*

37. *Jai Jai Jai Hanuman Gosain. Kripa karahu gurudev ki nyahin.*

38. *Jo sat bar path kare koi. Chhutehi bandhi maha sukh hoyi.*

39. *Jo yeh padhe Hanuman Chalisa. Hoye siddhi sakhi Gaureesa.*

40. *Tulsidas sada Hari chera. Keejai Nath hriday mein dera.*

Pavan tanay sankat harana mangala murati roop.
Ram Lakhana Sita sahita hriday basahu soor bhoop.

The Exploration

Doha 1: Establishing the Mind-Temple

श्रीगुरु चरन सरोज रज निज मनु मुकुरु सुधारि ।
बरनऊँ रघुबर बिमल जसु जो दायकु फल चारि ॥

Shri guru charan saroja-raj nija manu mukura sudhaari.
Baranau Raghubara Bimala Jasu jo dayaka phala chari.

Having polished my mind-mirror with the pollen-dust of my guru's feet.
I bask in the unblemished glory of the lord of the Raghu clan (Ram), bestower of life's four fruits.

Thus begins the Hanuman Chalisa, composed by Tulsidas four centuries ago in Awadhi, a dialect of Hindi spoken in the Gangetic plains around the cities of Awadh, or Ayodhya, and Kashi or Varanasi.

Chalisa means a poem of forty verses (chalis means forty in Hindi). Hanuman Chalisa, however, has forty-three verses. The main forty verses are chaupai, or quatrains (verses with four short, rhythmic segments). Framing these are three dohas, or couplets (verses with two long, rhythmic segments)—two at the beginning and one at the end—which serve as the entry and exit points into the 'mind-temple' that is created by the Chalisa.

Hindus have always believed that a temple can be created in the mind using words and verses, just as brick, wood and stone can be used to construct a temple in the material world. The psychological world exists parallel to the physical world; these are the two worlds inhabited by all living creatures (jiva in Sanskrit) according to Hindu scriptures. Only the non-living (ajiva) exist solely in the physical world.

In Hinduism, mind and matter are seen as interdependent, and their complementary nature was expressed using many words such as dehi-deha, atma-sharira, purusha-prakriti, shiva-shakti. The value placed on the psychological world is the reason why sacred Hindu writings are full of symbols and metaphors. The literal is for those who cannot handle the psychological, and prefer to see the physical as real. This yearning for the literal is indicative of insecurity, for the insecure mind finds it easier to control matter, which is measurable, than the mind, which is not.

The verse refers to the mind as a mirror that reflects the world. We think we engage with the real world, when in fact we engage with the world reflected in the mind-mirror. A dirty mirror will distort our view of the world, so we need to clean it. The cleansing agent is the dust of the guru's feet, who is so realized that the dust of his feet have the potency of pollen (saroj).

Our dirty mind-mirror is contrasted against the pure (vimala) glory of Ram who offers the four fruits (phala chari) that come from God, that nourish human existence: dharma (social order), artha (wealth and power), kama (pleasure) and moksha (freedom from material burdens).

Is there a relationship between the pollen of the guru's feet and the fruit bestowed by God? There could be. The mind which is a mirror (mukura) can also be seen as a flower (mukula), similar sounding words when we think about it. Is that deliberate device used by the poet? We can surely speculate. By the use of pollen-flower-fruit metaphors a connection is established between the guru's wisdom, a clear human mind, and the glory of the divine, which together will give us what we desire.

Having sought the blessings of the guru and invoked God, and polished the mind-mirror, it is time to declare the intention behind this enterprise we are embarking upon. It is time for the sankalpa.

Doha 2: Statement of Desire

बुद्धिहीन तनु जानिके सुमिरौं पवनकुमार ।
बल बुद्धि बिद्या देहु मोहिं हरहु कलेस बिकार ॥

Buddhi-heen tanu jannikay sumirow pavanakumara.
Bala buddhi bidya dehoo mohee harahu klesha vikaara.

Aware that I lack intelligence, I recollect the son of the wind god (Hanuman),
He will surely grant me strength, intelligence, knowledge and take away all problems and afflictions.

Sankalpa is the statement of purpose that marks the beginning of any Hindu ritual. We clarify who we are, and why we are doing what we are doing. This verse is the sankalpa that we are invoking Hanuman—identified here as the son (kumara) of the wind god (pavan)—to get what we want but don't have, and to rid ourselves of what we have but don't want. Thus the seed of desire is planted, with the hope of germination and fructification. Perhaps, the poet wants Hanuman to take care of him as Hanuman was taken care of by his divine father, the wind god Vayu, which is why he is addressing Hanuman using his father's name.

We identify ourselves as lacking intelligence (buddhi). In colloquial language, the one without buddhi is buddhu, a fool, and one with buddhi is either the intelligent (buddhiman) or the awakened one (buddha).

The Buddha is a title that was given to a prince who lived 2,500 years ago after he came to the conclusion that where there is life there is desire, and hence suffering. Suffering ends when we realize that nothing is permanent, neither the world, nor our sense of self. The ultimate aim is oblivion (nirvana) of the self which exists by imagining the world is real and permanent. The Buddha propagated this idea of dhamma (which is Pali for dharma) by establishing monastic orders (the sangha).

By contrast, Hinduism is life-affirming. Desire (kama) is accepted as the force that creates the world, with destiny (karma) as the counterforce that limits the satisfaction of desires. If one wants to give purpose to life, then it is to enjoy desire and accept destiny, without being addicted to either, and realizing there is more to life than satisfaction and suffering, desire and destiny. This can only happen when we have buddhi, complemented with strength (bala) and knowledge (vidya), which is what this chaupai refers to.

Strength without intelligence makes us dim-witted tools in the hands of others. Intelligence without strength, on the other hand, means we can never realize our dreams, for strength means a body that has stamina, a mind that has patience, and a life with access to resources and agency.

Knowledge without intelligence prevents us from being worldly. Intelligence without knowledge makes us narrow-minded, short-sighted frogs in a well. Knowledge is infinite, it has no boundaries, and in Hinduism, God is the personification of that infinite knowledge. Everyone has access only to a slice (bhaga) of reality; the one who knows all slices is God (bhagavan).

In the information age, as we move towards gathering data about everyone and everything, it is easy to assume we are moving towards infinite knowledge hence God-hood, through computers and databases. However, this data being gathered is material, not psychological. What is being measured is stimulus and its behavioural response. What is being manipulated by technology, is behaviour alone, not thought and emotions. What information is not being gathered is how the mind perceives and processes sensory stimuli. Science today is so focussed on the material, that it assumes measurable input (stimulus) and measurable output (behavioural response) is indicative of thought and emotion, and dismisses arguments to the contrary. Reality is seen as what we do (measurable), not what we feel (not measurable). At best, doing is seen as an indicator of feeling. At worst, doing is seen as relevant while feeling is considered of no consequence. When the West speaks of an intelligence quotient or an emotional index, it derives all understanding of the mind from measuring behaviour. Scientific is thus limited by measuring instrument. This distinguishes the modern discourse, and disconnects it with traditional Indian wisdom where measurement is seen as establishing delusion (maya) of certainty.

The obsession with quotients, and indices, hence mathematics, reveals the desire to control, regulate, manipulate human behaviour. Control, in Hinduism, is an indicator of fear. The intelligent seek control: the strong have the resilience to handle the lack of control, and the knowledgeable know the fultility of control. Hence, we ask Hanuman for strength as well as knowledge, along with intelligence.

We also ask Hanuman to solve our problems: problems that bother our mind (klesha) and problems that bother our body (vikara). Colloquially, klesha simply means a problem of any kind, but in Sanskrit 'klesha' refers to the psychological root of all problems such as lust (kama), anger (krodha), pride (mada), obsession (raga), revulsion (dvesha), jealousy (matsarya), that exists within us or in those around us. In the Bhagavad Gita, these kleshas are identified as vikara, making the two words synonyms. In Ayurveda, vikaras refer to diseases arising from the imbalance of the humours (doshas). Hanuman is being evoked to restore balance and harmony, in our mind and in our body, within us as well as around us.

Note that everything that is being sought from Hanuman involves the mind and body: we want him to give us strength, intelligence, and knowledge. We are not asking for fortune or success. With a healthy mind, we know, can cope with all of life's vagaries, and find happiness, always.

This doha marks the end of the introduction. Having paid obeisance to the guru and God, having made our statement of intent, we plunge into the main Chalisa, composed of forty chaupais.

Chaupai 1: Why Monkey as God

जय हनुमान
ज्ञान गुन सागर ।
जय कपीश
तिहुँ लोक उजागर ॥

Jai Hanuman
gyan gun sagar.
Jai Kapish
tihun lok ujagar.

Victory to Hanuman
who is the ocean of wisdom and virtue.
Victory to the divine amongst monkeys
who illuminates the three worlds.

In this verse, Hanuman is addressed for the first time by his most popular name, Hanuman, and identified as a monkey (kapi).

Classically, Hanuman means one with a wide or prominent or disfigured jaw, indicating a monkey. Colloquially, in the Hindi belt of India, the name means one without ego, pride and inflated self-image (maan), a meaning that makes sense when we appreciate the structure of the epic Ramayana, where Hanuman appears for the first time.

Some scholars have proposed that the word Hanuman comes from a proto-Dravidian word—an-mandi, which probably means male monkey—later Sanskritized to Hanuman. They also point to Hanuman being called Anuman in Thailand and Andoman in Malaysia, lands where Dravidian culture spread a long time ago. It has even been proposed that the Andaman Islands in the Bay of Bengal got its name from sailors who told stories of the great monkey who had the power to leap across the sea and reach distant islands. Those familiar with early Tamil Sangam literature dispute this theory.

The Ramayana reached its final form roughly two thousand years ago, and is one of the first epics to be composed in India with the intention of communicating Vedic ideas to the masses. It marks the birth of a new phase of Hinduism known as Puranic Hinduism, which is also marked by the rise of temple culture.

Before the Ramayana, for over a thousand years, maybe more, Vedic ideas were communicated using chants, melodies, rituals and conversations, not stories. This had a limited audience, the intellectual elite, such as priests, philosophers and aristocrats, with ample time on their hands. To reach out to a larger audience, Vyasa—the man who is credited with organizing Vedic hymns—composed the stories and epics compiled in the Puranas, including the story of Ram.

Some say Vyasa composed the stories himself, some say he compiled stories he heard from other sages, like Markandeya, and still others say he heard it from Shiva, or from the birds and fish who in turn had overheard the conversation between Shiva and Shakti. Amongst the birds was a crow called Kakabhusandi who told the story of Ram to the sage Narad who passed it on to the sage Valmiki, who transformed the story into the world's first poetry, which is why the Ramayana, the maha-kavya, is also called adi-kavya.

In the Ramayana, we find three sets of characters. In the north are the humans (nara) in Ayodhya, led by sages (rishis) who seek to enable humans to expand their mind, discover their divine potential (brahmana), which is the essence of Vedic wisdom. In the south, beyond the sea, on the island of Lanka are the demons (rakshasas) led by Ravana, son of a rishi (Vaishrava, son of Pulastya), who uses Vedic knowledge for power, and fails to internalize Vedic wisdom. In between, live the monkeys (vanaras).

Words like 'north' and 'south' in the Ramayana need to be read metaphorically, not literally, because Vedic thought is all about the mind, and seeks to inform how we 'see' the world. Ram is a metaphor. So is Ravana. So is Hanuman. The Ramayana takes place in the landscape that is our mind.

In nature, animals, including monkeys, compete for food, and so dominate and mark territories to secure their food. All behaviour is aimed at ensuring the body survives. This is the jungle way (matsya nyaya). To outgrow these animal instincts is the hallmark of humanity; it is our divine potential. To walk this path is dharma. But when we indulge in competition, domination and territoriality, we become worse than animals; we become demons, who subscribe to adharma. Ram embodies dharma. Ravana embodies adharma. Hanuman, from amongst all the monkeys, makes the journey towards Ram.

The world is composed of the self (sva-jiva) who lives in the ecosystem of others (para-jiva). For animals, monkeys included, the other is predator or prey, rival or mate. But humans have the ability to outgrow these hardwired animal instincts. The 'north' in the Ramayana is the highest potential that we can realize—where the self is not consumed by its own hunger for, and fear of, the other, but by empathy for other people's hungers and fears. This caring world is the world of Ram.

The 'south' in the Ramayana is where there is so much hunger and fear that the other is seen only as food and enemy, and the self (jiva-atma) twists itself and transforms into the ego (aham), unable to appreciate the divinity in the other (para-atma), hence the continuum of divinity that permeates the whole infinite universe (param-atma). This self-indulgent world is the world of Ravana.

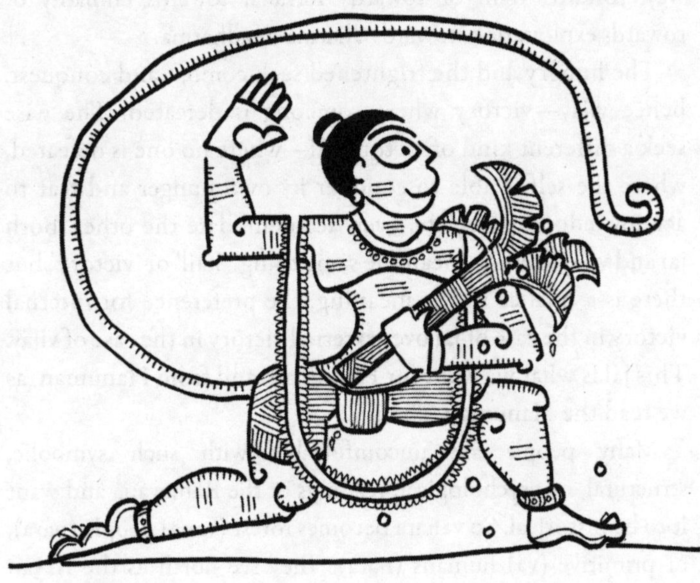

The rishis, who Ram defends, are sages who go from the north to the south to enable, empower and enlighten the hungry and the weak. They know that the other will see the sages from the north either as invaders or as patronizing benefactors, who seek to destroy their way of life. The rishis also know that should their wisdom slip, they will themselves be enchanted by the knowledge and power they are revealing.

Ravana, a son of one such rishi, embodies what can go wrong. Ravana uses his great strength, knowledge and intelligence to exploit those around him, be their lord and master, make them followers, rather than liberating them to find their own path. The liminal or in-between space between the north and the south is the land of the monkeys, our animal core, that can move either way, towards Ram or towards Ravana, towards empathy or towards exploitation, towards dharma or adharma.

The hungry and the frightened seek combat and conquest, hence vijay—victory where someone is defeated. The wise seek a different kind of victory, jai—where no one is defeated, where the self is able to conquer its own hunger and fear to acknowledge, appreciate, even accommodate the other. Both jai and vijay seem to mean the same thing, 'hail' or 'victory', but there is a nuance in the meaning, the preference for internal victory in the case of jai over external victory in the case of vijay. This jai is what we want for Hanuman, and from Hanuman, as we read the Hanuman Chalisa.

Many people are uncomfortable with such symbolic, structural, or psychological, readings of the Ramayana and want it to be historical. So vanara becomes forest (vana) people (nara), or primitive (va) humans (nara). They see north as the Aryan homeland in the Gangetic plains and the south as the Dravidian homeland south of the Vindhyas. Such rationalizations are often seen in people who are unable to differentiate the physical from the psychological, the measurable (saguna) from the non-measurable (nirguna), the form (sakar) from the formless (nirakar). Since the world is diverse, diverse readings of the Ramayana must be appreciated with empathy so that we appreciate the diverse needs of the human mind.

Chaupai 2: Son of Wind

राम दूत
अतुलित बल धामा ।
अंजनिपुत्र
पवनसुत नामा ॥

Ram doot
atulit bala dhama.
Anjani-putra
Pavan-sut nama.

Agent of Ram
Bearer of great strength.
Son of Anjani (mother)
Also known as son of the wind god (father).

This chaupai focuses on the origin and role of Hanuman. He is described as the son of the god of wind (Pavan) and a monkey woman called Anjana or Anjani, and has immense strength and uses his strength to serve as Ram's agent.

In the Vedas, divinity was often personified as natural phenomena: Indra, the god of thunder and Lightning; Agni, the fire; Soma, the juices within trees; Surya, the sun; Vayu, the wind. Pavan is a colloquial name for Vayu who is also known as Maruta, the god of storms. Pavan is also associated with prana (breath in the lungs) and vata (gases in the bowels), and so integral to life. The wind god who connects the earth with the sky is a companion and messenger of Indra, a role replicated by his son Hanuman, who is also known as Vayu-putra and Maruti.

If Hanuman gets his awesome strength from his father, his monkeyness comes from his mother, Anjana, a vanara woman. As the son of Anjana, Hanuman is often called Anjaneya, especially in South India. Not much is known about Hanuman's mother. In some stories, she was a nymph, an apsara, cursed to live on earth, after she upset a rishi. In other stories, she is the daughter of Gautama, the sage who discovers his wife, Ahalya, in the arms of Indra. She is cursed either by Gautama for not telling the truth about her mother or by Ahalya for not lying to her father. The curse involves her turning into a monkey. She marries Kesari, a vanara, who lives in Kishkinda.

The idea of a god making a human pregnant is often found in Greek mythology, where it is used to explain the existence of extraordinary heroes. Thus Hercules has a celestial father (Zeus) and a mortal father (Amphitryon) just as Hanuman has a celestial father (Vayu) and a mortal father (Kesari). Did this story of Hanuman have a Greek influence? At the time the Ramayana was being composed, Indian storytellers may have been exposed to Greek tales that had followed Alexander the Great to the East. We can only speculate as there is little by way of proof.

It is significant that Hanuman's father and mother are clearly identified. It means he is born of the womb (yonija). He is never referred to as self-created (swayambhu), indicating that his status is lower. In Hindu mythology, there are two kinds of gods: the greater ones who self-created and are hence beyond space and time, immortal and infinite, and the lesser ones who are born to parents and are hence located within space and time, are mortal and finite. In the Puranas, all old Vedic gods—Indra, Agni, Vayu, Surya—are given secondary status by being described as children of Kashyapa and Aditi. Primary status is given to Shiva and Vishnu who are described as self-created. Vishnu voluntarily takes a mortal form as Ram, thus striding both categories. Hanuman, however, does not fit so neatly into the second category: yes, he takes birth on earth, but he is also described as immortal (Chiranjivi). There are no stories of his death.

In the Mahabharata, Vayu places his seed in the womb of Kunti, as a result Kunti becomes the mother of Vayu's son, Bhima. While Vayu had chosen Anjani, Kunti had chosen Vayu. Kunti had invoked Vayu with a mantra, and asked him to give her a child, but Anjani had not. This made Bhima a child of desire, whereas Hanuman was a child of destiny.

As sons of the wind god, both Hanuman and Bhima are brothers. Like Hanuman, Bhima is very strong. But unlike Hanuman, Bhima is not divine. Bhima may be his elder brother's loyal agent, but that is not the same as serving Ram. For in serving his elder brother, Bhima does his duty as a younger brother, and is serving his family; in serving Ram, Hanuman is fulfilling no obligation but acting of his own volition and love. Bhima is as strong as Hanuman, but he lacks Hanuman's humility. While Hanuman is content being a messenger (doot) for Ram, as he is born of a monkey, Bhima feels entitled because he is born of a princess.

In Hindu mythology, destiny determined our body, our family, hence our social role. Our desire makes us either want to change a social role or cling to a social role. Destiny makes Ram the eldest son of a royal family, hence he acts as king. He does not desire to be king. Destiny makes Hanuman a monkey, he *chooses* to serve Ram, not for wealth and power, but for wisdom—the realization of the divine potential. Hence, he serves but does not seek. Bhima not only fulfils his social role, he also uses it to dominate the world around him, and benefit from his birth-determined strength and status. Hanuman teaches him to change his ways as we learn from the following story.

In his royal arrogance, Bhima always walked straight and expected all things to move aside and make way for him, even mountains and trees. Those who blocked his path were simply hurled aside or crushed underfoot. In his path, one day, he found an old monkey sleeping. 'I am too old to get out of your way,' the monkey murmured. 'Just kick my tail aside and make your way.' But when Bhima tried to kick the old monkey's tail, he realized it was really heavy, so heavy that it could not be pushed or pulled, even when he used all his strength. Bhima realized this was no ordinary monkey. When Hanuman revealed himself, he showed Bhima his awesome form (virat-swarup), making Bhima realize the insignificance of his physical strength and social position.

A king uses his power to serve people and create an ecosystem where people can outgrow hunger and fear. When a king uses his power to dominate those around him, it reveals the king has not outgrown his hunger and fear; he is not yet Ram. Likewise, a king's agent uses his power to serve his master. When a king's agent uses his power to dominate those around him, it reveals he has not outgrown his hunger and fear; he is not yet Hanuman.

Chaupai 3: Thunder Body, Lightning Mind

महाबीर
बिक्रम बजरंगी ।
कुमति निवार
सुमति के संगी ॥

Mahabir
Bikram Bajrangi.
Kumati nivar
sumati ke sangi.

Great hero
valiant, with Lightning body.
Who drives away bad thoughts
and is always accompanied by good thoughts.

Having explained his origins and role, this verse presents the qualities of Hanuman that make him worthy of worship. Most villages in India worship a vira, or hero, who protects the village. Hanuman is identified as Maha-vira, or Mahabir, who also protects the mind. Hanuman not only vanquishes physical demons like rakshasas and asuras, but also psychological demons such as negative thoughts (kumati) and ushers in positive thoughts (sumati).

Hanuman stands on the frontier between the wilderness and the settlement, between the animal and the human world, and has the power to turn the negative into positive, poison into medicine. This is why in temples Hanuman is often offered special Arka (*Calotropis indica*, Bowstring Hemp, Giant Milkweed) leaves and flowers, which grow wild in the forest and are poisonous. This 'negative' offering become positive after contact with his body.

Hanuman's status as a special kind of hero is reaffirmed by being called vikram, which is both a common noun meaning valiant and a proper noun referring to a legendary king, Vikramaditya, king of Ujjain, who was renowned for his worldly wisdom. There is a famous Sanskrit work known as *Vetala Pachisi*, which tells twenty-five tales in which Vikramaditya takes difficult decisions. These questions are posed by a ghost, or vetala, feared by all mortals, but not the brave king of Ujjain. Hanuman is like this legendary king, brave enough to face ghosts, and wise enough to solve complex puzzles.

Hanuman is also being addressed as Bajrangi, which means one who possess a body (anga) that is as powerful and radiant as the thunderbolt (vajra). In Hindu mythology, vajra is the weapon of Indra, the sky god who hurls thunderbolts against dark monsoon clouds to release rain. Indra once hurled this weapon at Hanuman and instead of being hurt by it, Hanuman simply absorbed and internalized his power. Hence he is also called Vajra-angi, one whose body is as powerful as a thunderbolt.

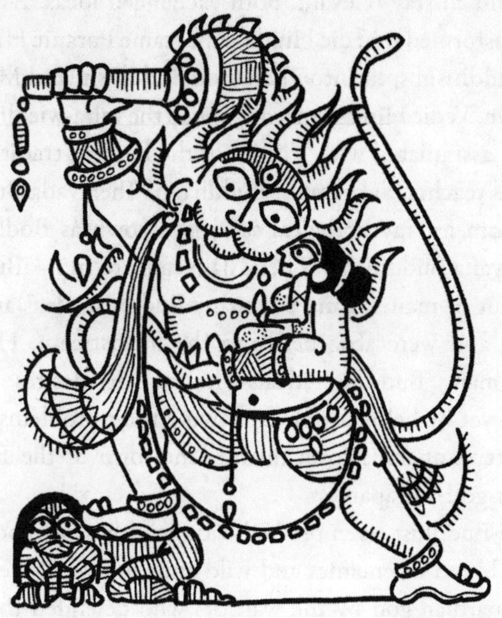

In Buddhist mythology, vajra refers to thunderbolt and diamond, and is a metaphor of incisive analytical abilities. Vajrapani is a guardian of the Buddha and a fearsome deity who strikes the ignorant down and grants the wise incisive, analytical abilities. He is visualized trampling the enemies of the Buddha and holding a vajra in his hand, much as Hanuman tramples demons and holds a mace in his hand, suggesting the overlapping roots of these two deities.

Vedic Hinduism, based on worldliness, thrived over three thousand years ago, but it was overshadowed, two thousand years ago, by Buddhism that valued other-worldliness. In order to spread, both Hinduism and Buddhism assimilated with folk beliefs and to stay relevant, both exchanged ideas. As a result both transformed—Vedic Hinduism became Puranic Hinduism, while Buddhism split into Theravada Buddhism and Mahayana Buddhism. Vedic Hinduism worshipped the vajra-wielding Indra who was assimilated with Vishnu of the Puranic tradition. The historical teacher, Sakyamuni Buddha, of Theravada Buddhism made room for mythological saviours known as Bodhisattvas of Mahayana Buddhism. When Islam came to India, Buddhism waned out of mainstream, but many Buddhist ideas and icons survived and were absorbed into the mainstream. Hanuman reflects many Buddhist ideals—he has no desires like the Buddha, yet he helps people by solving their problems like the Bodhisattva, and his form mirrors the form of the Buddhist guardian-god Vajrapani.

In pre-Buddhist, even pre-Vedic, times, it has been postulated that the blood of enemies and wild animals was offered to the village guardian-god by the warriors who defended the village frontier. Red became the colour of valour and fertility. Later, as the doctrine of ahimsa (non-violence) gained ground, blood was represented symbolically using sindoor (vermillion). Even later, the red colour was replaced by saffron colour, indicating celibacy and continence, a rejection of all things sensory. Buddhist monks were the first to use saffron, ochre, maroon and red robes to distinguish themselves from the robes of common folk, but eventually these colours were adopted by Hindu monks and saffron has now become the colour of choice of political Hinduism. Hanuman's orange-red body is often covered with silver and gold foil representing his Lightning-like body.

Chaupai 4: Darshan

कंचन बरन
बिराज सुबेसा ।
कानन कुंडल
कुंचित केसा ॥

Kanchan baran
biraj subesa.
Kanan kundal
kunchit kesa.

Golden body
seated with elegant adornments.
Rings in the ears
curly locks.

If the previous verse described the prowess of Hanuman, this verse focuses on his physical form: his golden complexion, his curly hair and his fine clothes, including the earrings.

The golden complexion reminds us that Hanuman is a monkey, with golden fur. But his earrings and curly hair draw attention to his humanity, as only humans wear ornaments and have hair on the head.

In some stories, Hanuman was born with earrings. The story goes that Vali, the king of monkeys, had heard that Kesari's wife Anjani was pregnant with a child who would be more powerful than him. So he cast a missile to hurt this child. However, instead of getting hurt, Vayu ensured the missile transformed into Hanuman's earrings, a symbol of Vali's, hence Indra's, defeat.

Earrings have a special significance in Hinduism. Piercing the ears of a child is a rite of passage (samskara). By piercing the ear, one creates a passage for sunlight through the body, making the body auspicious. Traditionally, men and women both wore earrings. So Vishnu is famous for his dolphin (makara) shaped earrings and Shiva is famous for wearing serpent (naga) shaped earrings. Hanuman's earrings connect him to fierce warrior-hermits known as Nath-yogi, of the ear-split (kan-phata) order (sampradaya), who were identified by their special earrings made of rhinoceros skin inserted by splitting the ear cartilage. Their gurus, Matsyendra-nath and Gorakh-nath, wrestled Hanuman and earned his respect.

Hanuman is described as well dressed. In folklore, he was born wearing an adamantine loincloth made of thunder, or diamond (vajra-kaupina), to reaffirm his celibacy, and his association with orders of ash-smeared, trident-bearing, warrior-hermits. This association with warrior-hermit orders starts only around a thousand years ago, following the institutionalization of the Hindu monastic orders, on one hand by wandering Tantrik mendicant jogis of the Nath order (such as Matsyendra-nath), and on the other hand by Vedantic acharyas such as Adi Shankara-acharya who established Hindu abbeys (mathas).

That the verse describes how Hanuman looks and what he wears indicates that we are gazing upon the deity. This is darshan, an integral ritual in Hinduism. The whole purpose of going into a temple is to see the deity and be seen by the deity, who invariably has large, shapely eyes that captivate the visitor even from afar. The devotee describes the deity's beauty, and hopes the deity will reciprocate, identify the devotee's needs and wants, and give them what they deserve and desire.

A Christian church, a Muslim mosque, a Buddhist monastery or a Sikh gurudwara are spaces designed to bring the community together and focus on a common goal—confess sins, reaffirm submission, awaken to desires and delusions and learn from the songs of the sages, as the case may be. But a Hindu temple is the house of a deity. We go to see them and be seen by them, no different from visiting a relative's or friend's house, or going to a king's court, with a petition.

The practice of invoking and adoring a deity and then petitioning him for material benefits informed the ancient Vedic ritual known as yagna. It continued to inform the later temple rituals known as puja. What makes puja different from yagna, however, is the value placed on darshan. The word 'darshan' has a double meaning: view as well as worldview, sight as well as insight. It is simultaneously about doing and thinking, action and introspection. It seeks to counter the purely intellectual approach of Buddhism where greater value is given to dhyan (meditation) wherein eyes are shut. It also seeks to appeal to the masses who are not interested in introspection. Deities in Buddhism are just tools to enable better meditation, while Hindu deities have elaborate form, their images, charged with hymn and ritual, are capable of responding to the prayers of the devotee. Darshan acknowledges the value of relationship, between deity and devotee, between self and other—in contrast to the isolation and individualism that informs Buddhist practices, and even Hindu monastic orders.

We prove that we have truly seen the deity on the basis of what offering we make. Every deity is unique and so seeks unique offerings. For Vishnu, there are tulsi leaves, for Shiva, there are bilva leaves. Hanuman is typically offered items sought by wrestlers and bodybuilders: til (sesame) oil, rai (mustard) oil, and urad (black gram) seeds, which build up muscle mass, and are traditionally considered 'hot' ingredients, firing up the body with energy.

Chaupai 5: Warrior, Servant, and Sage

हाथ बज्र
औ ध्वजा बिराजै ।
काँधे मूँज
जनेऊ साजै ॥

Hath bajra
aur dhvaja biraje.
Kaandhe moonj
janehu sajai.

You hold a thunderbolt club
and a flag in your hands.
And have the sacred thread
on your shoulder.

In the previous verse, the focus was on what Hanuman was born with—his complexion, his hair, even his earrings. This verse focuses on what he holds in his hands and bears on his body: a mace, a flag and a sacred thread (janehu) made of sabai grass (munja) on his shoulder. These are instruments (yantra) that embellish the icon (svarupa) of Hanuman and help refine our understanding of him.

The common word used for mace is gada, but the word used here is vajra, or the thunderbolt, which is Indra's weapon. In the Vedas, Indra is the greatest of gods, one who battles demons like Vritra, and releases the waters held by clouds. He is the patron of kings. Yet, in the Puranas, his role is reduced. He is the lord of Paradise (Swarga), leader of devas, who lives in celestial regions and enjoys worldly pleasures, but lacks wisdom. He needs the help of Vishnu to fight the demons (asuras) who lay siege to Paradise and declare war relentlessly. This shift in status indicates a shift from the older more materialistic Vedic way to the later Vedic (Upanishadic) way where greater value was placed on the mind (on meaning) than on riches and power.

In the Puranas, every deity has a flag (dhvaja) of his own—

Vishnu has a flag with the image of a hawk known as garuda-dhvaja, and Shiva has a flag with the image of a bull known as vrishabha-dhvaja—but Hanuman's dhvaja belongs to Ram, in keeping with his role as Ram's messenger and commander of his armies. Hanuman holds both Indra's weapon and Ram's flag, which endorses his status as mightier than the old Vedic celestial god-king, but serving the latter Puranic earthbound god-king.

Hanuman's janehu makes him a twice born (dvija). Hindus believe that we have two births: first there is physical birth and then there is the psychological birth. Physically, we are born out of the mother's womb into human culture. Our navel reminds us of our origin in the mother's womb. In Hindu culture, pierced earlobes are indicators of human culture, similar to the practice of tattooing, or tooth-filing, in other cultures.

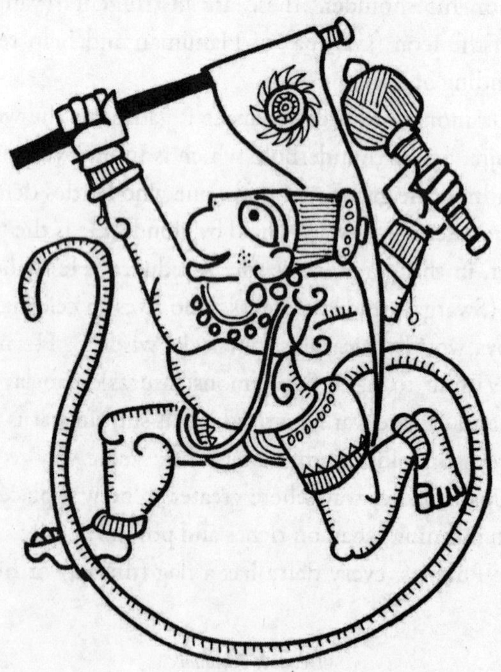

Our psychological birth takes place when we accept a guru who reveals to us the secrets of the Vedas. The mark of psychological birth is the sacred thread made of munja grass that hangs over the left shoulder. This thread has three strings representative of the Hindu trinity: Brahma, Vishnu, and Shakti. It also reminds us that while animals have only one body (physical), humans have three (physical, psychological and social). Hanuman accessed Vedic wisdom through Surya, the sun god, who also revealed Vedic secrets to Yagnavalkya, the sage whose words are captured in many Upanishads. Vedic secrets include knowledge of karma and dharma, of aham (our identity based on hunger and fear) and atma (our identity independent of hunger and fear).

Hanuman being given the janehu, despite being a servant of Ram and a wild forest creature, is not highlighted in the Valmiki Ramayana but becomes prominent in later texts, especially regional Ramayanas written in vernacular languages in the last five centuries, when caste excesses had peaked. People were asking: what makes a real Brahmin, effort or birth? Hanuman becomes Brahmin by effort and education, while Ravana is the son of a Brahmin named Vaishrava, who married a rakshasa woman, Kaikesi. The Vedas turn Hanuman from beast to human, giving him the wisdom and compassion to unconditionally help a man find his lost wife. By contrast, Ravana although human, and despite his Vedic knowledge, behaves like a brute, grabbing another man's wife for his own pleasure.

That Hanuman holds a weapon in his hand establishes him as a warrior (Kshatriya). That he holds Ram's flag establishes him as a servant (dasa, Shudra). That he has the sacred thread across his chest establishes him as a Brahmin, one who has accessed the Vedas. Thus the highest and the lowest stations of Vedic society (varna) are accommodated in Hanuman, a creature of the forest.

Chaupai 6: Rudra's Eleventh Form

संकर सुवन
केसरीनंदन ।
तेज प्रताप
महा जग बंदन ॥

Sankar suvan
Kesari nandan.
Tej prataap
maha jag bandan.

Shankara's (Shiva's) manifestation
Kesari's son
Your glory
is venerated by the whole world

This verse connects Hanuman to Shankara, which is another name for Shiva. For many devotees today, Hanuman is a form of Shiva. He is described variously as the son of Shiva, as the manifestation of Shiva, as an avatar of Shiva, as the eleventh Rudra form.

This connection between Hanuman and Shiva began roughly 1,500 years ago, a time that also saw Puranic Hinduism split between two schools of thought: the Vaishanvites who saw the world-affirming Vishnu as the supreme divine being and the

Shaivites who saw the world-renouncing Shiva as the supreme divine being.

When the Ramayana became popular, Vishnu-worshippers saw Ram as the mortal form (avatar) of Vishnu who kills Ravana, a devotee (bhakta) of Shiva. This turned the Ramayana into a tale of rivalry between Vishnu and Shiva. To counter this, Shiva-worshippers said that Hanuman was the form of Shiva. They pointed to Hanuman's status as brahmachari (celibate, continent and content, with no wants or needs) and his colour being as white as camphor (karpura-go-ranga) indicative of his being Shiva.

In some stories explaining the origins of Hanuman, it is said that when Shiva saw Vishnu in the form of Mohini, or Parvati, he began to sweat profusely. Vayu collected this sweat and poured it in the ear of Anjana, a vanara woman, who gave birth to Hanuman. Anjana's husband, Kesari, raised Hanuman as his own son and so Hanuman is also known as the son of Kesari. So besides a mortal father (Kesari) and a Vedic father (Vayu), Hanuman also has a Puranic father (Shiva). Besides a mortal mother (Anjani), Hanuman also has a celestial mother (Shakti).

According to Shaivites, Shiva himself descended as Hanuman to destroy Ravana, an errant Shiva-bhakta. According to them, Ravana had offered his ten heads to Shiva and obtained boons that made him very powerful. But as Rudra, Shiva has eleven forms. Ravana's offering of ten heads satisfied the ten forms of Rudra. The eleventh unhappy Rudra took birth as Hanuman to kill Ravana. Hence Hanuman is also Raudreya. In Maharashtra, the seventeenth-century saint Ramdas established eleven Maruti temples, reminding all of Hanuman's association with the eleven forms of Rudra.

To establish their superiority, Vishnu-worshippers argued that

Hanuman, hence Shiva, obeyed instructions given by Vishnu. To counter this, Shiva-worshipers said that without Hanuman's help, Ram would never have found Sita. In many retellings of the Ramayana, it is Hanuman who enables the killing of Ravana. For example, in one Telugu retelling, despite knowing that Ravana's life resided in his navel, Ram shot only at the head of Ravana as he was too proud a warrior to shoot below the neck. So Hanuman sucked air into his lungs and caused the wind to shift direction making Ram's arrow turn and strike Ravana's navel.

Hanuman's association with Shiva, and with celibacy, was reinforced by Hanuman's association with the various ascetic schools of Hinduism, including the Nath-yogis who followed the path of Matsyendra-nath from around 1,000 years ago, to the Vedantic mathas who followed Madhwa-acharya from around 700 years ago, and Sant Ramdas who inspired many Maratha warriors 400 years ago. The latter sages, especially during the Bhakti period, introduced the idea of connecting celibacy with service; you give up your worldly pleasures and work for the worldly aspirations of society. Just as the hermit Shiva became the householder Shankara for the benefit of Humanity, these sages spoke of how the ascetic Hanuman became Ram's servant for the benefit of society.

At one time, women were not allowed to worship Hanuman. By his mere radiance, it is said in many stories, he can make them pregnant. In the stories of Nath-yogis, one learns of queens who become pregnant by simply listening to the song of Hanuman, or fish becoming pregnant by consuming the sweat of Hanuman, for his radiance permeates into his voice and his sweat. As the centuries passed the overtly masculine nature of Hanuman was toned down. Just as Shiva was domesticated by Shakti, Hanuman's gentle side is evoked by Sita. Since there can be no Shiva without Shakti, many say that Shakti took the form of Hanuman's tail and always accompanied him. Hence, today women also worship Hanuman to solve their problems.

Chaupai 7: Clever and Concerned

विद्यावान गुनी
अति चातुर ।
राम काज
करिबे को आतुर ॥

Vidyavaan guni
ati chatur.
Ram kaj
karibe ko aatur.

Educated, virtuous
and clever.
Ram's tasks
you always do eagerly.

In the very first chaupai of the Chalisa, Hanuman is described as the ocean (sagar) of knowledge (gyan) and virtue (gun). This verse also reinforces Hanuman as being knowledgeable and virtuous, and adds that he is also clever (chatur). This tendency to complement one quality with another is a typical Indian idiom. Just as one spice does not create a dish, and just as a good curry is a clever combination of various spices, even a good person is a combination of various qualities.

In nature, we often say that the strong dominate the weak. But nature does not discriminate against the weak. They are given smartness to compensate for their physical weakness. Strength and smartness are tools to find food and security, to survive and thrive. Hanuman is strong *and* smart and thus has the best of animal qualities. His knowledge and virtue are what make him human and divine.

This verse reminds us that the educated man is not smart and the smart man is not educated. And a smart educated man is dangerous unless he has virtue. What is virtue? The ability to look beyond our own hungers and fears and be concerned of other people's hungers and fears. The way Hanuman behaves when he first meets Ram and Sita indicates how his knowledge, his cleverness and his virtue work together.

When he sees Ram and Lakshman wandering in the forest, looking for something, he realizes there is value in introducing them to Sugriv, the monkey-king. He approaches Ram, taking the form of a brahmin, and speaks in chaste Sanskrit, the language of the gods, which is an indicator that he has knowledge of the Vedas. Thus he evokes trust in the wary Ram, who is agonizing over the abduction of Sita.

Later, when it is time to meet Sita in Lanka, he wonders if he should speak in Sanskrit again while introducing himself. But he has seen Ravana speak in Sanskrit, and fears Sita will assume he is an imposter: Ravana's agent, or Ravana himself, posing as Ram's messenger. So he speaks to her in the organic language spoken by common folk. This is Prakrit (informal, organic language) as against Sanskrit (formal, designed language).

In neither situation is Hanuman trying to show off or intimidate the other with his knowledge. He is driven by concern for the other. He is not anxious of the other; he can sense the anxiety of the other. He is smart enough to anticipate how people react in stress: how they get startled at the sight of a stranger, and think the worst. The ability to adapt to the situation, and win the trust and confidence of both Ram and Sita through speech, reveals his sensitivity to people and to context, his communication skill, and most importantly, his empathy.

Chaupai 8: Other People's Stories

प्र्भु चरित्र
सुनिबे को रसिया ।
राम लखन
सीता मन बसिया ॥

Prabhu charitra
sunibe ko rasiya.
Ram Lakhan
Sita man basiya.

Ram's stories
you enjoy listening.
Ram, Lakshman
Sita as well, always reside in your heart.

For Hindus, one of the ways to expand our mind, and discover the divine within, is by listening (shravana) to stories of the divine.

Puranic stories are containers (patra) of Vedic wisdom (atma-gyan). Stories are of different types: memoirs (itihasa), chronicles (purana), epics (maha-kavya), narratives (akhyana), glories (mahatmya), biographies (charitra), songs (gita), prose-poetry (champu). Hanuman nourishes himself intellectually and emotionally by listening to stories of Ram, as we learn from this verse.

Traditionally, in gatherings where Ram's story is read out, one seat is always left vacant. Hanuman is described as rasika, one who enjoys the aesthetic juices (rasa) of Ram's tale. As per Hindu aesthetics, a good story is like good food. It needs to have multiple flavours that stir the senses and arouse emotions, for only then can it incept thoughts that can help expand the mind.

In folk tradition, Hanuman grows up listening to stories of Ram narrated by his mother. How is that possible? How can Hanuman hear stories of events that he himself participated in? In the Hindu worldview, the world goes through cycles of re-birth and re-death, just like any other living creature. In each of its lifetimes (kalpa), the world has four phases, like all living creatures: childhood, youth, maturity and old age. These are the four yugas, identified as Krita, Treta, Dvapara, and Kali. The Ramayana takes place in Treta Yuga. Since the world has gone through infinite lifetimes, and in each kalpa there has been a Ramayana, everyone in every age knows the story of Ram. Anjana narrates to Hanuman stories of Ram from an earlier kalpa.

Hanuman is so excited to hear the story of Ram that he desires to meet Ram. And so he goes to the city of Ayodhya where he learns that Ram, the prince, is craving for a pet. Hanuman lets himself be captured by the soldiers who gift him to the prince. That way Hanuman becomes Ram's pet and also spends his childhood as Ram's companion. Thus, in local oral traditions,

Hanuman is with Ram throughout his life, not just after Sita's abduction as narrated in various Sanskrit and regional texts.

In the Valmiki Ramayana, when Ram and Sugriv meet for the first time, they exchange stories. Ram tells him his tragedy, how Ravana abducted his wife. Sugriv tells him his tragedy, how Vali usurped his kingdom. Hanuman realizes that Ram's story has a solution for Sugriv's problem, and Sugriv's story has a solution for Ram's problem. If Ram helps Sugriv get his kingdom, Sugriv will help Ram find his wife. Listening to each other's stories reveals mutual benefit. Had stories not been shared, neither would the problem be understood nor would a solution have been found.

To see the other is to hear their stories. Brahma, the creator of all living organisms, and his children, such as Indra, are not worshipped because they do not care for other people's stories; they are consumed by their own. In exasperation, Shiva beheads

Brahma, which is why Shiva is called Kapalika. Shiva has learned the importance of storytelling from Shakti. Together they establish their relationship by telling each other stories, stories that overheard by birds and fish and shared with the rest of the world.

Vishnu hears the stories of Brahma's children, and nudges them to hear the stories of those around them. But reciprocity is not easy. By listening to Sugriv's story, Ram not only understands his problem, he also understands Sugriv's personality. He realizes that Sugriv sees him as an ally but has doubts. So Ram shoots a single arrow through seven trees, earning Sugriv's admiration and trust. Ram also realizes that after getting his kingdom, Sugriv will forget his end of the bargain, not because he is a cheat, but simply because he is so consumed by what he wants from others, that he is unable to see what others want from him. Still, he gives Sugriv the benefit of the doubt and helps him overpower Vali.

When Sugriv hears Ram's story, he sees a prince in distress and a potential ally in his fight against Vali. He sees what value Ram brings to him; he does not see Ram for what Ram is. By contrast, just by hearing Ram's story, Hanuman realizes that Ram is no ordinary human: his story has no villains, or victims, or heroes, just hungry and frightened humans seeking meaning. Hanuman recognizes Ram as the embodiment of divine potential, of atma, of dharma, all that is referred to in the Vedas, all that was taught to him by Surya.

Hanuman does Ram's darshan each time he hears Ram's story. He wants to participate in it, even as a minor character, for he relishes the idea of being part of Ram's story. One day, he narrated the story of Ramayana to his mother: how the monkeys and he built the bridge to Lanka, fought the rakshasas, killed Ravana and reunited Sita with Ram. Anjana was not impressed, for she felt her son was not living up to his potential. 'You could have just swung your tail and defeated the demons and rescued Sita without this whole charade of building a bridge and fighting a war. Why didn't you?' she asked. Hanuman replied, 'Because Ram did not ask me to.' Hanuman knew the Ramayana was Ram's story, not his. He did not want to control or appropriate or overshadow Ram's story. It was about Ram, not him.

It is significant that the very first narrator of the Ramayana is Hanuman himself: he describes Ram to Sugriv, he tells the story of Ram's adventures to Sita when he meets her in Lanka and does the same when he meets Bharat in Ayodhya. Later, he writes the first biography of Ram known as Hanuman Nataka, but destroys it so that Valmiki gets the credit of writing the first epic on Ram.

In stories, Hanuman observes Ram's relationship with Lakshman and Sita, and realizes how Ram's brother and Ram's wife complete him, and how he completes them. When Hanuman places all three of them in his heart, he is essentially placing in his heart the idea of relationship: that the self is incomplete without the other; that the self exists in an ecosystem of others. That is why in Hindu temples, no deity is placed alone: the deity always has a spouse, or a child, or a companion, or an attendant. Even Hanuman, who has no relatives, is not placed alone; we know that in his heart is present his master, who in turn is accompanied by his brother and his wife.

This value placed on relationship between the self and the other is key to Hindu stories. Most mythologies, ideologies and philosophies around the world can be broadly classified into two categories: individualistic and collectivist. Individualistic mythologies value the one over the group. Collectivist mythologies value the group over the one. Greek and Taoist ways, for example, are individualistic; Abrahamic and Confucian ways are collectivist. One can even classify Shaivite mythologies as individualistic and Vaishnavite mythologies as collectivist. However, that is not quite accurate. Hindu mythologies are best understood in terms of relationship: Shiva's relationship with Shakti and Vishnu's relationship with Lakshmi. Instead of the binary of the individual and the group, Hinduism focuses on the relationship between two individuals (the dyad). Shiva tends to withdraw from the other; Vishnu engages with the other.

When we relish the stories of the gods as Hanuman does, we see the gods truly, and recognize their presence or absence in us, just like Hanuman.

Chaupai 9: Adapting to Context

सूक्ष्म रूप धरि
सियहिं दिखावा ।
बिकट रूप धरि
लंक जरावा ॥

Sukshma roop dhari
Siyahi dikhava.
Vikat roop dhari
Lank jarava.

You took a small vulnerable form
before Sita.
You took a giant fearsome form
to burn Lanka.

In the first quarter of the Hanuman Chalisa, a lot of emphasis is placed on the origin, form and attributes, the role as well as the preferences, of Hanuman. We refer to his mother, his earthly and celestial fathers, we refer to his appearance and his symbols, his qualities and capabilities, his love for Ram's stories, and his desire to serve Ram.

With this verse we are describing his many feats: his ability to contract and expand himself physically as the situation demands. To the frightened Sita, he appeared as a small non-threatening monkey. To the arrogant Ravana, he appeared as a giant fearsome creature. Hanuman is thus no ordinary creature—he is a shape-shifter who knows what shape other people respond to.

In Hinduism, God is constantly playing games (leela) nudging the devotee-child to realize his divine potential. Thus God can expand or contract, encompass infinity (virat-rupa), and change shape and size for the benefit of all living creatures. Vishnu, for example, manifests as a fish, a boar, a priest, a king, or a cowherd. This ability to adapt for the benefit of the other is a hallmark of divinity, one that Hanuman also possesses.

The transformations of Hanuman described in this verse, of contracting and expanding in size, come from a chapter known as Sundar-kand in the Ramayana. The chapter is named beautiful (sundar) as it evokes hope: the possibility of Sita and Ram reuniting, thanks to the intervention of Hanuman. It is also thus named because it is the only place where he experiences the tenderness of Ram's love for Sita and Sita's love for Ram. Hanuman conveys Ram's words and describes Ram's sorrow to Sita, and Sita conveys her feelings to Ram through Hanuman, even sharing intimate secrets, such as how Ram used to rest his head on her lap when he was exhausted in the forest.

Hanuman's puny form makes Sita wonder how he could possibly have leapt across the sea. So Hanuman reveals his giant form and reassures her. Later, Hanuman lets himself be caught by Ravana's soldiers so that he gains an audience with the rakshasa-king. Hanuman is astute enough to realize that sensible words will not work with one such as Ravana who is consumed by his own self-importance, and is so frightened that he constantly feels the need to dominate those around him. Unable to break free from his animal nature, Ravana only understands the language of force. So when Ravana refuses to treat Hanuman as a messenger and give him due respect by offering a seat to him, Hanuman creates his own seat, extending and coiling his tail; only Hanuman's seat is at higher level than Ravana's throne, forcing Ravana to look up rather than down, a humiliation that Ravana cannot bear. Furious, unnerved, the king of Lanka orders his soldiers to set Hanuman's tail on fire. Hanuman responds by twirling his tail in every direction, setting fire to Ravana's beautiful palace and the city of Lanka around it, before leaping off the island-kingdom.

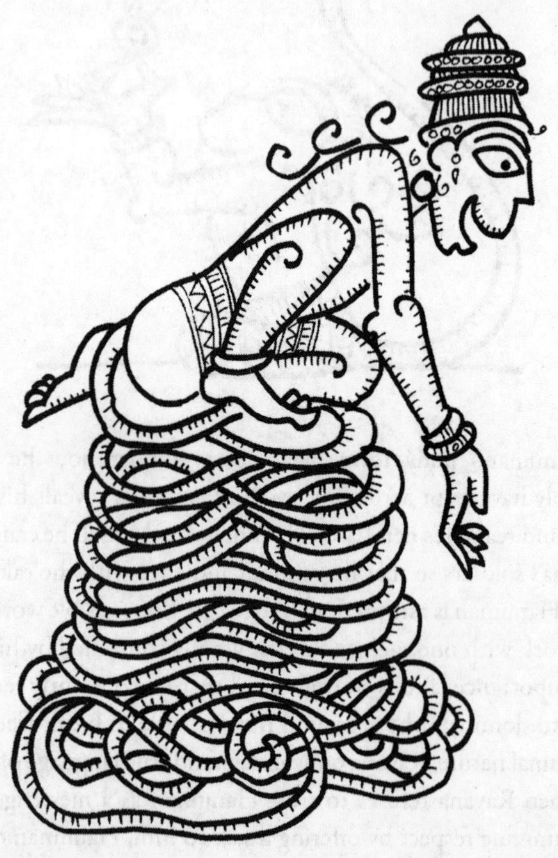

In India, there are broadly two types of monkeys—the red-faced monkey with golden fur and the black-faced monkey with silver fur. In folklore, it is believed that the soot of Lanka burning turned the red-faced monkey into the black-faced monkey.

In art, Hanuman images can be classified into two types depending on the location of the tail: if it is lowered, it indicates the gentle (saumya) form with which Hanuman approached Sita and Ram; if Hanuman's tail is raised, it indicates the fierce (rudra) form with which Hanuman stood up to Ravana. This reaffirms Hanuman's relationship with Shiva who is known for both his gentle (Shankara) and fierce (Bhairava) forms.

Hanuman is also depicted, especially in the south, with his arm extended as if he is going to slap someone. This is called 'tamacha' Hanuman: the form he took to humiliate Ravana. By contrast, when his image is placed next to Ram, his arms are in a position of veneration: this form is called Ram-dasa, the servant of Ram.

Chaupai 10: Demon-Killer

भीम रूप धरि
असुर सँहारे ।
रामचंद्र के
काज सँवारे ॥

Bhima roop dhari
asur sanghare.
Ramachandra ke
kaj sanvare.

You took fearsome forms
to kill demons.
Ramchandra's
tasks were thus accomplished.

A typical image of Hanuman enshrined in temples, shows him crushing a demon underfoot. Sometimes two demons—mostly a man, but sometimes a woman. These could be one of many demons that Hanuman overpowers in the Valmiki Ramayana and in the many regional and folk Ramayanas.

On his way to Lanka, Hanuman encounters three female demons—Simhika, Surasa and Lankini—who protect Lanka from intruders. Simhika has the power to capture her prey by its shadow; so she grabs hold of Hanuman's shadow and forces him into her mouth. Hanuman does not resist, he reduces himself in size so that rather than bite him, she is forced to swallow him. Inside her stomach, he expands in size and escapes by ripping out of her entrails, causing her to die.

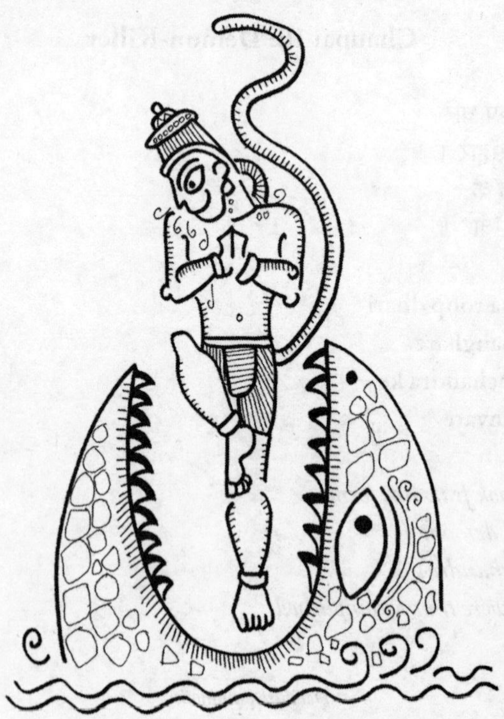

Surasa blocks Hanuman's path in the middle of the sea and tells him that he cannot pass until he enters her mouth; that is a boon she has been given by the gods. Hanuman has no choice but to enter her mouth. He increases his size forcing Surasa to widen her jaws. Then in a moment, he reduces himself to the size of a bee, and zips in and out of Surasa's mouth. Surasa has no choice but to let Hanuman pass for he has outwitted her with his agility.

While he first contracts and then expands to escape Simhika, Hanuman expands and later contracts to escape Surasa, the mother of serpents. While he uses brute force to kill Simhika, he uses cunning to escape Surasa.

In Lanka, Hanuman simply shoves the guardian-goddess of Lanka, Lankini, to the ground, making her realize he is no ordinary monkey, but the monkey destined to defeat Ravana. The defeat of Simhika, Surasa and Lankini marks the beginning of the end of Ravana's rule.

The female demon depicted under Hanuman's foot is sometimes interpreted as Lankini, Surasa or Simhika. Some identify her as Panvati, or a malevolent astrological force that causes misfortune. Others see her as Surpanakha (Ravana's sister), embodying the lustful woman who is the opposite of the celibate sage embodied by Hanuman.

Some see this fierce relationship of Hanuman with female demons as a rejection of Tantra where female deities preside and the focus is the acquisition of occult powers. In folklore, the celibate male ascetics (jogi) are often in conflict with sexually alluring female sorceresses (joginis). This is seen as reflecting the conflict between the austere, refined Vedanta tradition where the focus was wisdom and liberation, and the crude Tantra tradition where the focus was power and control.

Not everyone appreciates the idea of violence against women, even if the woman is a demon. In most images, the demon under Hanuman's foot is male and identified as Kalanemi sent by Ravana to prevent Hanuman from finding the Sanjivani herb, or Mahiravana who Hanuman outwits to save Ram from Pa-tala. The demon embodies obstacles that come in the way of success. Crushing him marks the crushing of obstacles. That is why Hanuman is called the remover of obstacles (sankat-mochan).

The mighty Hanuman is imagined sometimes with ten heads (dasa-mukhi) or with five heads (pancha-mukhi). In the latter form, the extra heads are those of other animals: a horse, lion, eagle and wild boar. These indicate Hanuman's association with wisdom (horse), valour (lion), vision (eagle) and tenacity (boar). It also visibly reveals Hanuman to be more than a monkey. This form of Hanuman is called Maha-bali, and is seen as standing independent of Ram.

Hanuman displays his cosmic form (virat-swarup) in various situations, in various contexts: to impress Ram when they meet for the first time, to inspire the monkey army as he leaps across the sea, to overpower Simhika, escape Surasa, defeat Lankini, to instil hope in Sita isolated in Lanka, to intimidate Ravana in his court, and finally, in the Mahabharata, to teach Bhima humility. But at all times, this mighty form of Hanuman contains his humility, the desire to serve Ram always.

Chaupai 11: Saving Lakshman

लाय सजीवन
लखन जियाये ।
श्रीरघुवीर
हरषि उर लाये ॥

Laye Sanjivan
Lakhan jiyaye.
Shri Raghuvir
harashi ur laye.

By fetching the Sanjivani herb
you saved Lakshman.
Scion of the Raghu clan
hugged you in delight.

In the Ramayana, the rakshasa-king Ravana abducts Sita and takes her away to the south across the sea to the islandkingdom of Lanka. To save Sita, her husband Ram and Ram's brother

Lakshman take the help of the vanaras to build a bridge to Lanka and declare war against Ravana.

In the war that follows, Ravana's son Meghnad, also known as Indrajit, strikes Lakshman with a deadly arrow containing the venom of serpents. Lakshman loses consciousness and risks losing his life as the poison begins to spread through his limbs. Only a herb called Sanjivani can save Ram's brother, if applied to the wound before sunrise the next day. But the herb grows on a mountain far away in the north, who can fetch it from so far, so soon? Ram wonders as the sun begins to set.

The vanaras shout, Hanuman, of course! Did he not leap across the ocean and reach Lanka as if jumping from one branch of a tree to another? Surely, he can fly north and bring back the herb in one night. Ram looks at Hanuman with anxious eyes, his heart filled with deep despair at the thought of his dying brother. In response, Hanuman turns north and jumps.

As Hanuman rises to the sky, Ravana catches sight of him, and figuring out his mission, summons the magician Kalanemi and orders him to create obstacles so that Hanuman does not find the herb, and even if he does, he does not return before sunrise.

Kalanemi uses his magic to reach the Dronagiri mountain where the Sanjivani grows before Hanuman and waits there disguised as a hermit. On Hanuman's arrival, he welcomes him with words of praise and offers him food. Hanuman finds it inappropriate to say no to an offer of hospitality so he accepts the invitation, but insists on taking a bath before the meal. So Kalanemi directs him to a pool full of crocodiles. Hanuman not only takes a bath, he also kills the crocodiles when they attack him. The crocodiles turn out to be apsaras, celestial damsels cursed by Indra to live on earth as reptiles until liberated by a monkey. They thank Hanuman and reveal Kalanemi's true identity. A furious Hanuman attacks and strikes Kalanemi dead.

Much time has been lost, it is now the middle of the night and Hanuman has no time to find the herb on the mountain. It's too dark. So he picks up the entire mountain and flies back south to Lanka. Just as he is nearing Lanka he observes that the sun, goaded by Ravana, is being made to rise before his time. So with his free hand he grabs the sun, traps him in his armpit and makes his way to Ram, mountain in hand.

The herb is found, Lakshman is saved and the sun god released to rise, much to Ram's relief and delight. This very popular event from the Ramayana is described in this chaupai.

Hanuman with Kalanemi underfoot and Sanjivani in his hand is the form in which he is worshipped in most temples. Kalanemi represents the obstacles in our life. Sanjivani is the solution to our problems. The image captures the idea behind the worship of Hanuman—he removes obstacles and solves problems, which is why he is adored by all. Hanuman embodies the pragmatic aspect of Hinduism, quite different from the philosophical side.

There are many other stories of Hanuman carrying mountains, not linked to Sanjivani. The vanaras, we are told, carried many mountains from the Himalayas to build the bridge to Lanka. When the construction of the bridge was complete, all the vanaras were told to drop the mountains they were carrying wherever they were. All the mountains we see in the southern part of India, it is said, have their origin in the Himalayas and were brought south by the vanaras. The mountain being carried by Hanuman was called Govardhan. He felt bad that he would not see Ram. So Hanuman promised Govardhan that in a future birth, Ram would surely see him. So Ram took birth as Krishna in the Dvapara Yuga, and grew up on the slopes of Govardhan and even lifted him up with his little finger.

Chaupai 12: A Brother Like Bharat

रघुपति कीन्ही
बहुत बड़ाई ।
तुम मम प्रिय
भरतहि सम भाई ॥

Raghupati kinhi
bahut badai.
Tum mam priye
Bharat-hi-sam bhai.

Ram sings
praises of you.
'You are as dear to me
as my brother Bharat.'

Ram is so thankful for Hanuman's many interventions that enable him to succeed in his mission and so touched that Hanuman asks for nothing in return, except the pleasure of serving him, that he cannot stop himself from praising Hanuman and declaring that he is as dear to him as his brother, Bharat.

This comparison is significant. Bharat is the son of Kaikeyi, the second wife of Ram's father Dashrath whose machinations led to Ram being forced into exile in the forest for fourteen years. Bharat, however, refused to be king in Ram's place. He did not appreciate his mother's ambitions and deceit. He begged Ram to return to the palace, but Ram refused as he had given his word to his father that he would stay in the forest for fourteen years. So Bharat returned to Ayodhya, placed Ram's footwear on the throne, and ruled the kingdom as Ram's regent until his return.

By comparing Hanuman to Bharat Ram elevates the status of Hanuman from servant to family. This indicates a significant elevation of Hanuman's status and his inclusion in Ram's heart. One cannot help but wonder if this narrative elevation of Hanuman is not political, an attempt by wise men of society to bridge the inequality, without threatening the old system: a calculated counter-force of wisdom that keeps the default social force of hierarchy in check.

In Eknath's Marathi Ramayana, when a childless Dashrath conducts a yagna for a son, he receives a magic potion from the heavens that he gives to his three wives who bear him four sons. A hawk grabs some of the potion and carries it to the jungle and puts it in Anjani's mouth. The son she gives birth to may be a vanara, but he is very much a brother of Ram, Lakshman, Bharat and Shatrughna.

In a folk variant of the Ramayana, when Hanuman is flying with the mountain southwards towards Lanka he passes Ayodhya. Fearing he is a rakshasa who intends to drop the mountain over the city, Bharat strikes Hanuman with an arrow causing Hanuman to descend. A duel is averted when Bharat identifies himself as Ram's regent and Hanuman reveals that he is Ram's servant. Hanuman then proceeds to tell Bharat the tragedy that has befallen Ram and how Ram is fighting Ravana to rescue his wife, Sita. The narration takes a long time. Hanuman suddenly realizes that the sun will soon rise and he is far away from Lanka. He fears he will not reach on time. So Bharat tells Hanuman to sit on his arrow, mountain in hand. He then fires the arrow, thinking of Ram, and the arrow takes Hanuman to Lanka in a fraction of a second, just in time to save Lakshman's life. Thus Bharat and Hanuman collaborate to save Lakshman and make Ram happy. Hanuman is thus included in the royal family of Ayodhya.

Chaupai 13: Vishnu's Avatar

सहस बदन
तम्हरो जस गावैं ।
अस कहि
श्रीपति कंठ लगावैं ॥

Sahas badan
tumharo jasa gaave.
Asa-kahi
Shripati kanth lagaave.

May thousands
sing your praises.
So saying
Shri's husband (Ram) hugs you.

With this verse begins the praise of Hanuman. Until now, we have focussed on the origin, the form and the feats of Hanuman. Now, we list all those who admire Hanuman's glory.

Ram tells Hanuman that thousands of beings will praise him. Here, Ram is identified as Shri-pati, lord of the goddess of fortune, meaning Vishnu. In which case, the thousands who praise Hanuman could refer to Adi-Ananta-Sesha, the cosmic serpent with thousands of hoods on whose coils reclines Vishnu, on the ocean of milk.

The linking of Ram to Vishnu means that Ramayana is being acknowledged as a subset of the Vishnu Purana, which in turn is a narrative expression of the Vedas.

In the Vedas, Vishnu is a minor deity, a younger brother of Indra, his companion, but he has nothing to do with preserving the world. He becomes a major deity—the preserver and protector of the earth—later in Puranic liteature. In the Vedas, the king is identified with the conquering Indra and the moral Varuna, but in the Puranas, the king is identified with Vishnu, especially in the form of Ram, and Varuna is the god of the sea, father of Lakshmi, the goddess of fortune. Lakshmi chooses Vishnu as her guardian and consort. She manifests next to him as the embodiment of tangible assets (Bhu) and intangible value (Shri).

Sita of the Ramayana, is Lakshmi of the Puranas, who is Shri of the Vedas. The word 'Shri' is found in the Rig Veda, the oldest collection of Hindu hymns (mantra), over 4,000 years old, where it refers to affluence and abundance. In the Shri-Sukta, the goddess of fortune is invoked for grain, gold, cows, horses, children, wealth and health. The word 'Shri' also happens to be the first word in the Hanuman Chalisa, found in the very first doha, even before the word 'guru'. Some people believe that the guru being referred to in the doha is Sita herself, who is seen as Hanuman's guru in some Shakta traditions. Thus, while Vaishnavas see Hanuman as Vishnu's servant, and Shaivas see him as a form of Shiva, the Shaktas or Goddess worshippers saw Hanuman as a student of the Goddess, and Ram as the consort and guardian of the Goddess.

The Vishnu Purana informs us that Lakshmi was churned from the ocean of milk, a metaphor for domesticating and cultivating the forest. The division between the forests (aranya) and in the settlement (grama) is first found in the Sama Veda. In the Shiva Purana, the forest is Kali, mother of humanity, and the village is Gauri, daughter of humanity. Brahma is the creator, who turns forest into field, turns nature (prakriti) into culture (sanskriti)—where human rules apply.

However, the world created by Brahma is full of conflict and sorrow. His children, the devas and the asuras constantly fight each other. And so Brahma is not worshipped. Instead, prayers are offered to Shiva, the hermit, who rejects wealth and power, and withdraws from society, and returns to the jungle for peace. Shiva, the opponent of Brahma, is therefore described as the destroyer. Brahma's world brings prosperity but no peace. Shiva's world brings peace but no prosperity.

Vishnu, the preserver, stands in between Brahma and Shiva. He gets Brahma's quarrelling children to collaborate and churn Lakshmi out of the ocean of milk. Thus, like Brahma, he engages with society and generates and enjoys wealth, but unlike Brahma or his children, he does not see himself as the controller of Lakshmi. Instead, like Shiva, he has inner peace not to crave control over the wealth he generates. He freely and fairly distributing it with detachment. This makes him Lakshmi's ideal husband. He protects her, enjoys her, but does not seek to control her. That is why Vishnu is called Lakshmi-vallabha, the beloved of Lakshmi, and Shri-pati, lord of wealth.

Vishnu descends on earth and takes various mortal forms, such as Ram, to show humans how to live life, generate, enjoy and distribute wealth without getting addicted to it. He speaks of dharma, the human ability by which the self (sva-jiva) can make room for the other (para-jiva), thereby creating a society where there is both prosperity and peace. This combination of abundance and happiness constitutes the idea of Shri. Because he makes this happen, Vishnu (hence Ram) is identified as Shri-pati.

Chaupai 14: Brahma and his Mind-born Sons

सनकादिक
ब्रह्मादि मुनीसा ।
नारद सारद
सहित अहीसा ॥

Sankadhik
Brahmaadi muneesa.
Narada-Sarad
sahita Aheesa.

Sanak,
Brahma, and other sages.
Narada, Saraswati,
alongwith the lord of serpents.

In the previous verse, Ram who is Vishnu praises Hanuman. In this verse, praise is being showered by Brahma, and the sages.

Brahma is the creator-god of Hinduism, but never worshipped. Creation in Hinduism does not mean creator of material things, but creator of self-identity (aham) and seeker of divine identity (atma). This creation happens on the canvas that is nature.

In nature, there are non-living things (a-jiva) and living organisms (sa-jiva). The living have awareness of death, and hence yearning for life, hunger for food and fear of becoming food. In humans, this hunger and fear is amplified. We imagine a world where there is ample food and no threats. Failure to get this world creates sorrow. We feel like victims, and are filled with self-pity. The creator of these emotions is not worshipped in Hinduism.

The destroyer of these emotions is worshipped in Hinduism. The creator of aham brings sorrow (dukkha). The destoyer of aham, the embodiment of atma, brings joy (ananda).

Happiness comes from knowledge, embodied as the goddess known as Saraswati, here referred to as Sharada. The sages (muni), including Sanaka and Narada, mark the struggle to acquire this knowledge. They worship Hanuman, as they recognize that Hanuman has this knowledge. Hanuman has this knowledge because he has genuinely seen Ram, recognized him as Vishnu, the embodiment of dharma, who has outgrown his own hunger and fear, and empathizes with other people's hunger and fear, and so is always in a state of ananda, despite huge calamities.

The first of Brahma's sons were the Sanat-kumars. They have various names such as Sana, Sanaka, Sanata, Sananda. Typically, they are visualized as four prepubescent boys. In the Puranas, sexual activity must not be taken literally: the male form represents the mind and the female form represents matter. The attraction of a sage for a nymph is a metaphor for the response of the mind to sensory stimuli. Prepubescent boys means they do not have the wherewithal to engage with the world, or even desire it. They wander everywhere seeking the wisdom that will bring happiness. As long as they don't grow up, and engage with the world, the knowledge will elude them. But they don't know that and so wander through space and time, never growing up or old.

Narada, born after the Sanat-kumars, is an adult, capable of engaging and desiring the world. However, he chooses not to be part of the material world, and goes around telling all living creatures that living in the material world is full of hunger and fear and suffering, and has no meaning, until he is cursed by Brahma that he will never escape the material world unless he gets everyone to engage with it. For unless one engages with the world, experiences hunger and fear, one will never outgrow hunger or fear, never gain empathy or find meaning. In other words, without the material, there can be nothing spiritual.

Saraswati is called Sharada because Sharada was the name of a popular script in India about a thousand years ago, used to write the Vedas, before the Devanagari script became popular. Brahma wants to possess her, and when he does that, she runs away from him, and Shiva beheads Brahma. Knowledge has to be internalized, transformed into wisdom, not memorized. Brahma is beheaded because he chooses the path of the brahmin (crumpled mind that seeks to dominate others using his knowledge and position) rather than the path of the brahmana (expanded mind that internalizes the Vedas and so feels no urge to dominate).

The Aheesha mentioned in this verse refers to the lord of serpents (naga), just as Kapisa mentioned in the first chaupai refers to the lord of monkeys. It can refer to Vasuki, king of serpents, who rules the nether regions. It could refer to Adi-Ananta-Sesha, on whose hoods rests the earth. Or it could refer to the serpent Kundalini, coiled at the base of our smile, embodying our primal survival instincts, which can rise up and stir the flowering of wisdom in our mind, turn knowledge into wisdom. In wisdom, we see the world for what it is, rather than trying to control the world like Brahma and his children, and being trapped in hunger and fear and meaningless, we become like Ram, and Hanuman.

When Hanuman was a child, he did not know his strengths. He picked up boulders and mountains, trees and elephants, as if they were toys and hurled them around. So the sages declared that Hanuman would lose all memory of his great strength. It would reveal itself as needed. Every time Hanuman faced a crisis, or needed to solve a problem, he became aware of his hidden strengths and talents. In other words, the serpent of wisdom slowly rose up his spine, making him increasingly aware of the world, and the context, so that he could decide wisely how to make use of his incredible natural strength. Eventually, his great strength enabled him to leap across the oceans and carry mountains across land. But thanks to his teacher Surya, and thanks to his experience of Ram, he was able to transform knowledge into wisdom, use Saraswati not to cling to wealth (which is a mark of hunger) or dominate others (which is a mark of fear), but to outgrow his hunger and fear. This is why everyone adores him—Brahma, and his sons, the sages, even the goddess of knowledge and the serpent of wisdom.

Chaupai 15: Admirers in Every Direction

जम कुबेर
दिगपाल जहाँ ते ।
कबि कोबिद
कहि सके कहाँ ते ॥

Jam Kubera
Digpaal jahan te.
Kavi kovid
kahi sake kahan te.

Yama, Kubera
other guardians of the directions
Poets as well as scholars
cannot praise you enough

While the Hanuman Chalisa enables immersion into the idea of Hanuman, it also expands our understanding of the Hindu worldview. In this verse we are being introduced to the idea of Digpaal, or Digga-pala, the guardians of the sky who are located in eight spots: the four cardinal and the four ordinal directions. Here Hanuman's popularity is being reaffirmed. Even the guardians of space are singing praises of Hanuman, as are the poets (kavi) and scholars (kovid).

As the Puranas came to be composed, the Hindu universe came to have a unique architecture. The world was seen as a lotus flower, with continents spreading out like petals from a central mountain called Meru. The continent on which India is located is called Jambudvipa, stretching from the Himalayas to the oceans, and watered by seven rivers; it is the land of the blackbuck. Spreading over it like a canopy is the sky, pegged at eight different locations: north, south, east, west, northeast, northwest, southeast and southwest. At each peg is located a guardian (Digga-pala) and a pair of elephants (Digga-gaja).

The north is marked by the Pole Star, and is the land of permanence. This makes the south the land of impermanence, ruled by Yama, the lord of death. In the south rules Ravana, the king of rakshasas, who drove his elder brother Kubera, king of yakshas, to the north. If Ravana lives in Lanka, Kubera lives in Alanka, or Alaka. If Ravana grabs the fortune of others, Kubera, as the lord of treasures, gives fortunes to others. Metaphorically, the two directions counter each other. Yama fills life with fear while Kubera fills it with hope. Life is a combination of fear and hope. Both these deities complement each other, and both praise Hanuman.

Other Digga-palas include Indra on the east and Varuna on the west, who also complement each other: Indra embodies fresh water of rain while Varuna embodies saltwater of the sea. The ordinal directions are marked by the sun complemented by moon, and wind complemented by fire. These gods of space praise Hanuman. He is being adored in all directions.

Many Hanuman temples declare themselves to be Dakshina-mukhi, with Hanuman facing the south, the direction of death and decay. In this, Hanuman mimics Dakshina-murti, the south-facing form of Shiva found in South Indian temples. This form of Shiva is called the teacher of teachers as he gives discourse on the Vedas, Tantras, Nigamas and Agamas for the benefit of sages. But Dakshina-mukhi Hanuman is more ferocious than intellectual; he protects devotees from rakshasas, demons who reside in the south. This is not the literal south, but the metaphorical south.

One can say it refers to the negative impulses in our body, located in the lower part of the brain. One can say it refers to our base instincts or the base instincts of others, such as jealousy and rage that wreak havoc in relationships.

Hanuman has a special relationship with poets and scholars. Poets respond to the world with their heart, scholars with their head. Both adore this warrior monkey-god. Why? Because Hanuman is one of them: a poet and a scholar, and there are many stories testifying to that.

His love for knowledge is evident when he begs the sun god, Surya, to be his teacher, and reveal to him the secret of the Vedas. He does not mind suffering the glare of the sun while he is studying.

His love for storytelling is revealed when he narrates the story of Ram (Ram-katha) first to Sita in Lanka and later to Bharat in Ayodhya. In these narrations, he describes Ram using the most beautiful words and phrases. Hanuman's love for music is revealed when Narada, the musician-sage, watches him melt ice on the Himalayas with the sheer power of his singing the praise of Ram (Ram-bhajan).

Chaupai 16: Enabling Sugriv

तुम उपकार
सुग्रीवहिं कीन्हा ।
राम मिलाय
राज पद दीन्हा ॥

Tum upkar
Sugrivahin keenha.
Ram milaye
rajpad deenha.

Eternally grateful to you
is Sugriv.
You introduced him to Ram
who made him king.

This chaupai draws our attention to events in Kishkinda that led to Sugriv becoming king, thanks to Hanuman's intervention, with the help of Ram.

As stated earlier, the story of Ramayana draws attention to the state of affairs between three worlds: Ayodhya, where humans (manava) uphold dharma; Kishkinda, where monkeys (vanara) reside and struggle with dharma; and Lanka, where barbarians (rakshasa) reside and ignore dharma completely. Vanaras are thus located between the world of dharma and adharma.

In dharma, you give in order to get, and accept whatever you receive. In adharma, you grab whatever you want, as there is no concept of, or regard for, personal property. In between these two worlds is the world where you give and *take*: you are bound by obligations to fulfil. This is the world where you demand fair exchange, where fairness is not spontaneous, but enforced, through law or force. This is demonstrated in the politics of Kishkinda.

The king of Kishkinda, Riksha, once fell into a pond and turned into a woman. Two gods fell in love with his female form: the rain god Indra and the sun god Surya. From his union with the two gods, Riksha had two sons: Indra gave him the mighty Vali, and Surya gave him the meek Sugriv. Riksha, who had been both father and mother to the two brothers, asked them to share the kingdom equally after his death.

All was well until there was a misunderstanding. A rakshasa attacked Kishkinda and in the attack that followed, Sugriv assumed that Vali had been killed. But Vali had been victorious, and saw his brother's hasty conclusion as indicative of his guile and ambition. Rather than sort out the mistrust, and re-establish faith, Vali drove Sugriv out of Kishkinda by force and claimed the kingdom for himself. He made Sugriv's wife, Ruma, part of his harem. In other words, Vali behaved like a typical alpha male monkey who corners all the foraging lands and females of the troop for himself.

Had Hanuman not intervened, Vali would have killed Sugriv.

Hanuman was a student of the sun god and had been asked by the sun god to take care of his son Sugriv; and Hanuman had promised to protect him. Hanuman observed that Vali wanted to kill Sugriv and Sugriv survived by hiding atop Rishyamukh mountain—the one place that Vali feared to go. A sage had once cursed Vali that if he ever stepped on this mountain, he would die. So Vali, determined to hurt Sugriv, would fly over the mountain and kick Sugriv on the head. When Hanuman saw this happening day after day, he decided to stop Vali. He caught Vali's leg and threatened to drag him to the mountain top to perish. Vali begged for mercy and Hanuman let him go after threatening him with a slap (resulting in the icon known as 'tamacha' Hanuman) and extracting a promise: Vali would quit his petty behaviour and let his brother be. If Hanuman wanted, he could have hurt, even killed Vali. But he did not, as he had no quarrel with Indra's son. In other words, he did not interfere in the Sugriv-Vali conflict and focussed on taking care of Sugriv, as instructed by his guru.

It was Hanuman who spotted the jewels that Sita cast down to mark a trail as she was being taken to Lanka by Ravana on his flying chariot, the Pushpak-viman. This led Hanuman to Ram and Lakshman who were moving south in search of Sita. He introduced Ram to Sugriv. He felt the two could help each other: Ram could help Sugriv become king of Kishkinda and Sugriv could help Ram find Sita.

While Hanuman had sensed Ram's nobility and valour, Sugriv had no faith and wanted proof of Ram's talent as an archer. Ram had to shoot an arrow through seven trees, convincing Sugriv that he was indeed a worthy ally. Sugriv then challenged Vali to a duel and while the two were fighting, Ram who was hiding behind the bushes shot Vali dead with his arrow.

Vali condemned this act as cheating and Ram argued, 'One who does not know how to share, or forgive, one who lives by the jungle way, and uses his might to establish his authority, should not condemn the use of cunning in a duel, for that too is the jungle way, available for the survival of the meek. Besides, if I challenged you to a duel, by the ways of the jungle, Kishkinda would be my kingdom, not Sugriv's.'

Thus, with Ram's help, Sugriv became king. But when it was time to fulfil his end of the bargain, Sugriv said, 'Let's wait until the rainy season ends, travelling in the rain is dangerous.' While Ram waited patiently, Sugriv indulged in the pleasures of his harem, for even Vali's wife Tara was now his. He forgot all about his promise to help Ram even after the rains ended. Finally, an angry Lakshman decided to force Sugriv to help. 'I shall kill the cheat if he refuses to help,' declared Ram's brother. It was Hanuman who sensed trouble and restored peace. While he got Tara to calm the angry Lakshman down, he went to

Sugriv and told him to mend his ways, and keep his promise. Sugriv finally saw sense, apologized to Ram and organized his troops to find Sita.

Thus it was Hanuman who not only protected Sugriv from Vali's wrath but also enabled Sugriv to become king with Ram's help and protected him from Lakshman's outrage. Hanuman got Sugriv to follow the ways of dharma—not just take, but also give. Ideally, Sugriv should have helped Ram without any reminding or nudging. Hanuman had to remind Sugriv of his obligations.

While Lakshman expected Sugriv to keep his end of the bargain, Ram had no such expectation. For Ram was a yogi, who knows a man has rights only to action, not to the results of action. Only Hanuman noticed this and wanted to be the servant of the man who had no desire to be anyone's master.

Chaupai 17: Empowering Vibhishan

तम्हरो मंत्र
बिभीषन माना ।
लंकेस्वर भए
सब जग जाना ॥

Tumharo mantra
Vibhishan maana.
Lankeshwar bhaye
sub jag jana.

Your counsel that
Vibhishan accepted.
Made him Lord of Lanka
as the world knows.

This verse reveals the difference between the Valmiki Ramayana, composed 2,000 years ago, and Tulsidas's Ram-charit-manas, composed 500 years ago, and draws attention to the many variations found in regional and folk retellings of Ram's tale. While everyone acknowledges Valmiki as the first poet to compose the Ramayana, the epic itself has been reimagined, and retold, in many ways in various Sanskrit plays, Prakrit compositions, and—from about tenth century onwards—in various regional languages.

The difference between the oldest work and the later compositions is of two kinds. First, is the theme: while the focus of the Sanskrit epic was dharma and the obligations of a royal prince, the focus on the regional epics came to be bhakti and the veneration of a deity by his devotees. The second is the change in plot.

In the Ram-charit-manas we find an episode that is not found in the Valmiki Ramayana: the meeting of Hanuman and Vibhishan when Hanuman visits Lanka in search of Sita. Hanuman finds a man chanting Ram's name in Lanka. It turns out to be Ravana's younger brother. After introductions are exchanged, Hanuman informs Vibhishan that Ram is coming to Lanka to set things right. Vibhishan then directs Hanuman to the Ashoka garden where Sita has been confined.

Vibhishan does not agree with his brother's action of abducting another man's wife and imprisoning her in his garden. There are many reasons for this. There is the moral reason of respecting a woman's consent. There is the ethical reason of respecting another man's wife. Then, there is the practical reason: Ravana's actions damage Lanka's reputation and threaten Lanka's security. There is also the dharma reason: a king's misbehaviour affects the welfare of the entire kingdom. Vibhishan wants his brother to see sense and Hanuman urges Vibhishan to have a talk with his brother.

Unfortunately, Ravana does not like Vibhishan's arguments and protests and kicks his brother out of Lanka. Hanuman gives Vibhishan the courage to take a decision to override his deep love for his brother, and join forces with Ram.

Vibhishan reveals the various secrets and weaknesses of Ravana that enables Ram to defeat the rakshasa-king. And so in popular lore, Vibhishan is not respected. He is seen as a traitor, a disloyal brother. He is contrasted with Kumbhakarna, another of Ravana's brothers who shares Vibhishan's stance in the matter of Sita's abduction, but remains loyal to Ravana. He attacks Ram and is brutally killed by Ram's army of monkeys in the battlefield. The question emerges: is loyalty superior to dharma? For Ravana, the one who grab's another man's wife, is no follower of dharma.

Kubera, the king of yakshas and elder brother of Ravana, was the one who built the city of Lanka. Ravana drove Kubera out of Lanka and made himself king. Thus Ravana behaved as animals do, using force to establish his authority. This action is an even greater tragedy because Ravana is no barbarian; he is a Brahmin well versed in Vedic knowledge. But he misuses Vedic knowledge to dominate and exploit the world. In other words, he is not interested in the fundamental theme of the Vedas—atma-gyan, or self-awareness, which enables humans to outgrow animal instincts and empathize with the world.

Hanuman gives Vibhishan the strength to choose dharma over

loyalty. Loyalty indulges the self-image at the cost of the other. It values reputation of the self (sva-jiva) over the welfare of the other (para-jiva). Dharma is all about the other. It is what defines our humanity.

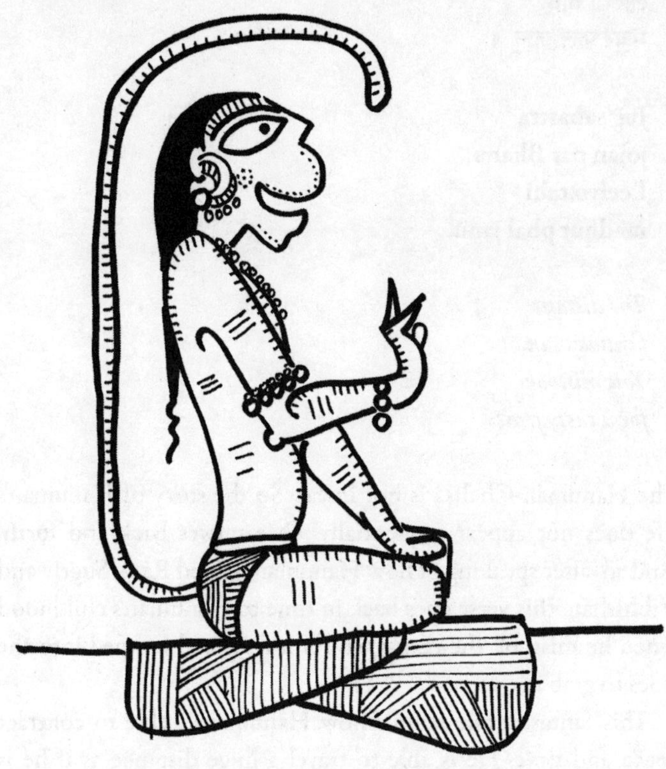

After the defeat of Ravana, Vibhishan marries Ravana's widow and becomes king of Lanka. He rules as a good king should—taking care of his people, rather than getting people to take care of him.

Chaupai 18: Sun as Fruit

जुग सहस्त्र
जोजन पर भानू ।
लील्यो ताहि
मधुर फल जानू ॥

**Jug sahastra
jojan par Bhanu.
Leelyo tahi
madhur phal janu.**

*The distant
faraway sun.
You mistook
for a tasty fruit.*

The Hanuman Chalisa is not linear. So the story of Hanuman's life does not appear sequentially. One moves back and forth. And so, after speaking of how Hanuman helped Ram, Sugriv and Vibhishan, this verse goes back in time to Hanuman's childhood when he mistook the rising sun for a fruit and jumped into the skies to grab it.

This fantastic tale reveals how Hanuman is able to contract space and time. He is able to travel a huge distance as if he is jumping across the branch of a tree. And he is able to consume the vast fiery ball that is the sun as if it is a fruit.

Some people have taken the phrase 'jug sahastra jojan' to refer to the distance between the earth and the sun, proof therefore that ancient India knew how to calculate distances in space using observation. They have taken jug or yuga to mean 1,200, sahastra to mean 1,000 and jojan or yojan to refer to 8 miles (approximately 13 km). So the line, they suggest, means roughly 150,000,000 km, in other words, the distance of earth from the sun. However, yuga refers to traditional time measurement (an era), and jojan refers to a traditional distance measurement. When you multiply the two you get speed, not distance. Such interpretations, however appealing, are misleading. It simply refers to Hanuman's ability to bend space and time, to not only reach the sun but also consume it by increasing his relative size. Hanuman does this as a child, without any training, without any knowledge of his own strength.

This is when the gods panic and Indra, god of the sky, hurls his thunderbolt at Hanuman, causing him to come crashing down to earth, disfiguring his jaw, giving him his name—Hanuman. But Vayu gets annoyed at the way Indra treats his son and hides in a cave with his son, until the gods beg Vayu's forgiveness and ask him to leave the cave and enable all creatures to breathe once again. In exchange, Indra and all the gods bless Hanuman with many powers.

In some stories, during his journey to the sun, Hanuman assumes all the other celestial bodies (grahas) and the constellations (nakshatras) to be toys and tosses them around. Hindus believe that the location of the grahas, relative to each other and relative to the nakshatras, provides the map of human destiny. The purpose of astrology (Jyotish) is to appreciate this cosmic pattern. Hanuman has the power to change the location of these celestial bodies, hence the power to change human destiny. The sun impacts our radiance, the moon impacts our emotions, Mars our aggression, Mercury our intelligence, Jupiter our rationality, Venus our creativity, Saturn our patience, Rahu our clarity and Ketu our calm.

People pray to Hanuman on Tuesday and Saturday so that he ensures the grahas exert positive, not negative, influence. The verse tells us how for Hanuman the flaming ball of the sun is equivalent to a juicy fruit. We also know how he held the sun in his armpit, and some say his mouth, while finding Sanjivani. Hanuman is therefore considered a force that can change our destiny, influence the power of the grahas, remove their malevolent influence and enable their benevolent influence.

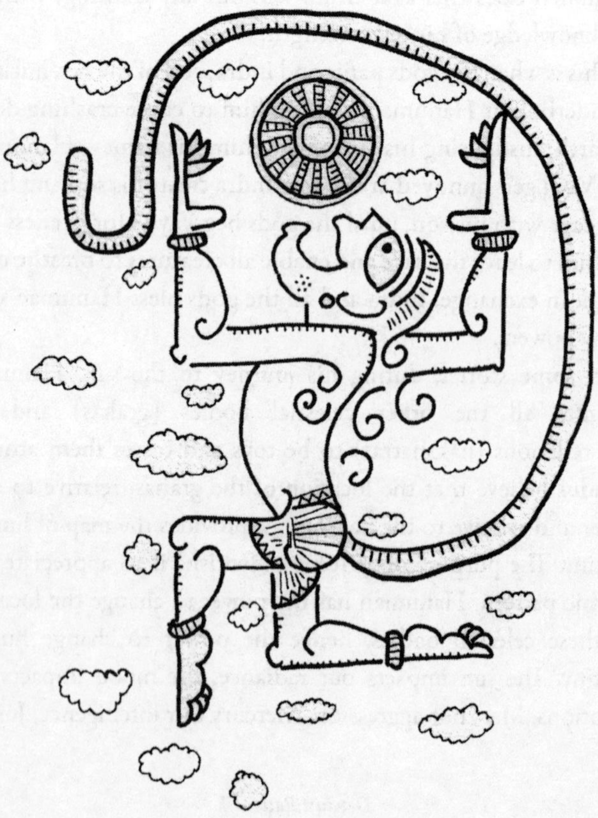

The sun god is also Hanuman's guru. Hanuman wanted to learn everything that there was in the world. He was advised to go to Surya, who sees all things. But Surya refused to be Hanuman's teacher arguing that he was busy travelling all day and at night he had to rest and so had no time to teach. Hanuman then began flying in front of the sun's chariot, facing the sun, suffering his glaring heat, determined to learn whatever the sun god could share during his daily journey from the east to the west. Impressed by this display of determination, the sun—who is lord of all grahas—taught Hanuman many things, amongst them how to counter the ill effects of dangerous planets, plants and animals. Therefore, one prays to Hanuman in times of crisis.

In the Ramayana, Ravana is a great astrologer who wrote the Ravana-samhita, a treatise on astrology. But he did this to figure out a way to manipulate the stars and planets to grant him fortune. Hanuman does not seek fortune. And he uses his strength to limit the malevolent influence of celestial bodies, and to give humans the strength to cope with the malevolent influence of celestial bodies. For Ravana, the sun has to be controlled. For Hanuman, the sun is a toy who entertains, and a teacher who enlightens.

Chaupai 19: Monkeyness

प्रभु मुद्रिका
मेलि मुख माहीं ।
जलधि लाँघि
गये अचरज नाहीं ॥

Prabhu mudrika
meli mukh mahee.
Jaladhi langhi
gaye achraj nahee.

With Ram's ring
in your mouth.
You leapt over the sea
how amazing is that.

Being knowledgeable and wise does not stop Hanuman from popping Ram's ring in his mouth while leaping over the sea. Mundane rules of propriety make no sense to Hanuman, reminding us of his animal side. His monkeyness evokes his childlike nature. In this, he reminds us of Bholenath, the guileless, innocent form of Shiva. This form of Hanuman is often addressed as Balaji, or the child-like form of Hanuman.

Hanuman's paradoxical qualities mirror the paradoxical qualities of Shiva. Both are wise and mighty, yet both are totally unaware of worldly ways. Shiva may have the power to destroy the three worlds (which is why he is call Tripurantaka) and enlighten the sages on the wisdom of Vedas and Tantras (which is why he is called Dakshina-murti), but he does not know how to function as a husband, a father, or a son-in-law, and has to be taught the ways of a householder by his patient wife, Parvati. Likewise Hanuman, who can leap over the sea with a mountain in hand and the sun in his armpit, does not know the value, and status, of a king's ring and does not understand why humans find his act of keeping Ram's ring in his mouth inappropriate.

The concept of 'value' exists only amongst humans. For

animals, food has value. For humans, an object becomes valuable based on what meaning we attribute to it. Meanings are given randomly. They are cultural: of a set of people, by a set of people, for a set of people, making no sense to outsiders or non-humans.

For example, the idea of contamination by the touch, saliva or even shadow of a person from certain communities, to establish the draconian caste hierarchy of India, of making some communities the embodiments of pollution in order to make other communities embodiments of purity. In the Ramayana, Lakshman is horrified when Shabari offers him berries after tasting them to check if they are sweet; he considers the food contaminated, but Ram has no problem eating the berries for he rises above such cultural meanings and is able to recognize that they exist in context and are not universal. What makes sense in one culture may not make sense in another. This discomfort with contamination following contact with saliva is implied in the verse where Hanuman casually puts Ram's royal ring in his mouth.

The ring is nothing special; it is simply a tool by which Sita can identify a messenger sent by Ram. It is the clever Hanuman who asks Ram to give him something by which he can win Sita's trust, for he can foresee a captive Sita being too insecure to trust him only on the basis of his words of instruction. For the poet, Ram's ring has much greater sentimental value, which makes little sense to a monkey whose focus is more pragmatic: finding and rescuing Ram's beloved.

Once, Sita gave Hanuman a string of pearls. He kept biting the pearls as if they were nuts. The residents of Ayodhya laughed at this, exclaiming that a monkey could not know the worth of pearls. When asked to explain his behaviour, Hanuman said, 'I was biting to see if Ram resides in these pearls. He doesn't, so they are useless to me.' The people found this to be an absurd idea, for Ram sat on a throne and could not be seated inside pearls. But Hanuman was surprised at their assertion and confidence. He just tore open his chest and there within his heart was Ram with Sita by his side. Suddenly, the people of Ayodhya realized what Hanuman was innocently drawing their attention to. For him, a thing had value if it was either food, or if it evoked divinity. He saw no value in expensive, royal pearls—for they neither nourished his body, nor his mind, as Ram did. Possessing pearls could make people rich. But engaging with Hanuman could make people experience what it meant to be Ram.

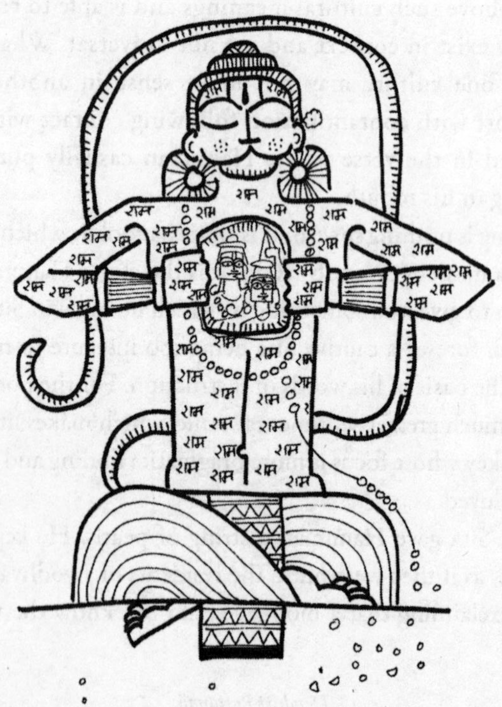

Just as humans give value to things, we also give value to gestures. Animals recognize only two kinds of gestures—those that threaten their security, and those that assure them of security. Humans, however, have complex gestures to establish hierarchy that are beyond Hanuman's understanding, for he does not understand the need for hierarchy when one has experienced Ram.

Once Narada told Hanuman that he had to bow to all the sages who paid a visit to Ram, everyone except Vishwamitra, who did not like anyone bowing to him. Hanuman complied, not knowing that this was Narada's trick to create a rift between Hanuman and Ram. Vishwamitra saw this as an insult and demanded that the monkey be killed. So Ram raised his bow and shot arrows at Hanuman. Hanuman simply chanted Ram's name—and such was the power of Ram's name that it created a force field that even Ram's arrows could not penetrate. Everyone bowed to Hanuman who showed the world in his very innocent way, that the *idea* of Ram is greater than Ram the king.

Thus, as the verse reiterates, Hanuman amazes you with his many incredible qualities—his ability to leap over an ocean, rip his chest open, resist Ram's arrows by chanting Ram's name. Simultaneously, he amazes you with simian innocence—holding Ram's royal ring in his mouth, biting pearls, trusting the mischievous Narada. This reminds us that Hanuman has no desire to impress anyone. His knowledge and powers exist to help others, materially and spiritually; else he is happy being monkey.

Chaupai 20: In Southeast Asia

दुर्गम काज
जगत के जेते ।
सुगम अनुग्रह
तुम्हरे तेते ॥

Durgam kaj
jagath ke jete.
Sugam anugraha
tumhre tete.

All tough jobs
in this world.
Become easy
with your grace.

A few years ago, Indian media went abuzz with the news that Barrack Obama, former President of the United States of America, carried, amongst many things, an image of Hanuman in his pocket. On closer examination, it turned out to be not the image enshrined in Hindu temples of India, but the image of Hanuman popular in Thailand. Hindus who see this image will not feel the same emotion they feel on seeing a Hanuman image from India.

Be that as it may, Hanuman grants everyone the psychological strength to cope with crises, which makes solving problems easier. Even an exiled Ram was able to raise an army of monkeys, build a bridge across the sea, defeat Ravana and his army of demons, and rescue Sita, with Hanuman by his side.

This story of Hanuman's ability to solve problems travelled beyond Indian shores on merchant ships travelling to Southeast Asia, which Indians knew as the golden land, or Suvarnabhumi. It is said that on the long sea voyages, sailors created the art of shadow-puppetry projected on the ship's sail using leather dolls, to tell the story of the Ramayana. Hence, along the coast of India and in many islands of Southeast Asia one finds this art form even today. In Thailand, the old capital was called Ayutthaya, the local name for Ayodhya, and the kings were seen as descendents and embodiments of Ram. The Southeast Asian Ramayanas include the Hikayat Seri Rama of Malaysia, Yama Zatdaw of Burma, and Ramakien, the national epic of Thailand. In these epics, one encounters a local version of Hanuman.

There are three differences between the Hanuman of India, and the Hanuman of Southeast Asia. First, the Ramayana mingles and merges with the local Buddhist lore of the regions. Second, the Hanuman depicted in these regional epics is a more strong and clever and funny monkey; loyal to Ram, but not quite a wise devotee, suggesting that the stories reached there from Indian shores over a thousand years ago, before the widespread popularity of the Bhakti doctrine. Third, Hanuman is not necessarily depicted as a celibate brahmachari or yogi; he is a charming rake, and a powerful warrior who battles demons and is able to satisfy the demonic desires of rakhasa women including Ravana's sister, Surpanakha, and his wife, Mandodari.

In the Vedas, there is a ribald argument between Indra and his wife Indrani over a huge male monkey, Vrishakapi, who happens to be Indra's friend. The conversation deals with Indra's lack of virility, Vrishakapi's excess virility, and Indrani's frustrated desires. It ends with the journeys and sacrifice of the monkey who restores Indra's power and Indrani's fertility. Some people postulate that this Vedic Vrishakapi transforms into the Ramayana's Hanuman. Details of his potent sexuality were rejected in India where society preferred a Hanuman with control over his senses, emotions, and desires. However, this idea may have travelled to Southeast Asia where Hanuman is known for his humourous erotic adventures.

There are many stories of Hanuman that are unique to Southeast Asian retellings. In one story, he battles the mermaid queen Suvarna-maccha (golden fish) who tries to disrupt the building of the bridge across the sea to Lanka. In another story, Benyakai or Benjkaya, the daughter of Vibhishan, uses her magical form to appear like the dead body of Sita washed up on the shores; Hanuman senses mischief and decides to cremate the 'dead body', which suddenly comes alive as the flame rises and runs away. When Ravana tries to break the bridge to Lanka, he expands in size and stretches his tail so that Ram and the army of monkeys can cross to Lanka with ease. These tales remind us how Hanuman, even in other lands, makes the toughest jobs look easy, even fun.

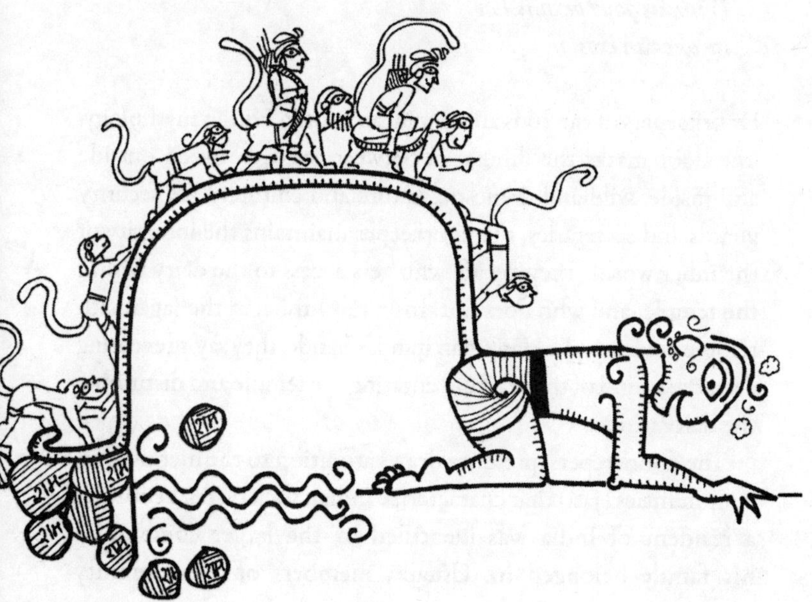

Chaupai 21: Doorkeeper

राम दुआरे
तुम रखवारे ।
होत न आज्ञा
बिनु पैसारे ॥

Ram dwaare
tum rakhvare.
Hoat na agya
bin paisare.

Ram's door
has you as guardian.
Without your permission
no one can cross it.

Doorkeepers of the gods are very important in Hindu mythology. The door marks the liminal in-between space between outside and inside, wild and domestic, nature and culture. Like security guards and secretaries, the doorkeeper maintains the integrity of the inner world. They decide who gets access to the deity within the temple, and who does not. In Puri, Odisha, at the Jagannath temple, for example, Hanuman stands outside, they say, preventing even the sound of the sea from entering the temple and disturbing the deity inside.

The doorkeepers' presence draws attention to the hierarchy of communities (jati) that characterize Indian society. For centuries, a resident of India was identified by the larger community his family belonged to. Usually, members of a community followed one profession. Each jati isolated itself, like most tribal communities around the world, by not permitting marriage with outsiders, thus protecting its knowledge system, which was its source of income. About 500 years ago, Europeans who visited India used the word 'caste' for jati, as it reminded them of the clan system in Europe where blood purity mattered greatly.

There are over 2,000 jatis in India today. For centuries, people have been trying to classify these into a fourfold hierarchy (chatur-varna), with Brahmin priests at the top, powerful landowners after them, followed by rich traders and the rest below. But what makes the jati system unique is not the economic and political hierarchy, but the concept of purity: some communities are seen as intrinsically pure (priests, for example), while others as intrinsically impure (janitors, butchers, undertakers, for example). The 'impure' were denied access to temples, kitchens, and even the community well. Thus, in a grand temple, only the pure could access the inner shrine where the deity was enshrined, while the impure ones had to stay outside, outside the door, at times even outside on the street.

Those who were not allowed to enter the temple, naturally, turned to Hanuman whose image was located outside the temple, at the entrance, or even on the street. He was far more accessible than the royal Ram, who sat deep within the complex, accessible only to the elite.

Hindu history reveals a long tension between the hierarchy of purity imposed by priests and the doctrine of atma revealed by the poet-saints. The latter doctrine led to the ritual of the gods going out on processions regularly, stepping out of the temple on palanquins and chariots, to meet those communities who were not allowed inside the temple. It also led to many doorkeepers being made to look very much like the deity enshrined within the temple. This was to assure those being excluded that while humans may exclude humans, God excludes no one.

The doorkeepers of Vaikuntha are called Jaya and Vijaya. The doorkeepers of the sacred groves of the Goddess are called Maya and Laya. Nandi the bull is Shiva's doorkeeper and vehicle (vahana). Hanuman is Ram's doorkeeper, messenger, secretary, and strongman.

Once Ravana paid a visit to Shiva but was stopped by Nandi at the door as Shiva was with Shakti, and the couple wanted privacy. Ravana did not like being stopped, and without heeding Nandi, tried to get past him. When Nandi blocked Ravana, Ravana called Nandi a monkey. Nandi did not appreciate Ravana's rudeness, for he was only carrying out his duty. He cursed the arrogant Ravana that monkeys would be the cause of his downfall. To make this happen, it is believed, a portion of Shiva's divinity manifested on earth as Hanuman. Nandi, the doorkeeper of Shiva, was avenged through Hanuman, Ram's doorkeeper, who defeated Lankini, Ravana's doorkeeper.

With Hanuman guarding the gates of Ram's palace in Ayodhya, even the god of death, Yama, feared entering the city when it was time for Ram to leave his mortal body and return to Vaikuntha. Finally, Ram moved Hanuman from the gates so that Yama could do his duty. Ram dropped his ring in a crack in the palace floor and requested Hanuman to fetch it. Hanuman entered the crack in the palace floor in the form of a bee, only to discover it was a tunnel leading to the land of serpents (Naga-loka) where he found a mountain made of Ram's rings. He wondered what was the secret. To this Vasuki, king of the nagas, said, 'The world goes through cycles of birth and death just like all living creatures. Just as every life has a youth, so does the world have a Treta Yuga when Ram rules the world. In this yuga, each time, a ring falls from Bhu-loka to Naga-loka, a monkey follows it, and Ram up there dies. As many rings as there are Hanumans and Rams. Nothing lasts forever. But what goes, always comes back.'

In north India, temples of many mountain goddesses who are manifestations of the tiger-riding Sheravali are guarded by Bhairo-devata and Langur-devata, the former looks like a child-warrior who drinks bhang (a narcotic), the latter looks like a monkey who drinks milk. Both these deities embody domesticated masculinities, the principles of brahmacharya (celibacy, continence) and yoga (inward orientation). Nowadays, many identify the Langur-devata with Hanuman.

Chaupai 22: Guardian of Fortune

सब सुख
लहै तुम्हारी सरना ।
तुम रच्छक
काहू को डरना ॥

Sub sukh
lahae tumhari sarna.
Tum rakshak
kahu ko darna.

All joy
exists in your shelter.
With you as guardian
there is nothing to fear.

This verse seeking shelter and protection from Hanuman evokes humanity's most primal needs. Every village in India had a guardian-god (vira) who protected the village from danger: wild animals and raiders. He or she protected the settlement (kshetra-pala). Hanuman emerges from the kshetra-pala tradition. He protected Sugriv, and he protected Ram, and he protects Ayodhya.

The idea of submitting to a divine being and seeking his shelter is prevalent in most religions. However, the reasons are different.

A Buddhist surrenders (sharanam) to the Buddha, as he seeks freedom from a world of suffering. A Christian seeks shelter in the love of Christ, as he abandons his way of sin and returns to God's fold. A Muslim submits to Allah, promising to live by His commandments revealed by His final prophet, Muhammad. These ideas informed the idea of submission in the Bhakti period of Hinduism.

The Hindu devotee submits (sharanagati) to either Ram, or to Shiva or Shakti who are worshipped by Ram, or to Hanuman, who worships Ram. The object of adoration (aradhana) could be all of them simultaneously, or each one of them sequentially, depending on need and mood. This complication arises because Hinduism is not monotheistic and does not seek to be monotheistic unlike most religions and doctrines. It acknowledges the diverse needs of people, and so the need for different deities for different people, each form being seen as one of the myriad manifestations of the divine.

In Hinduism, unlike Buddhism or Christianity or Islam, submission does not mean following a particular doctrine or a set of rules. It is submitting to the will of the divine, which in earlier pre-Bhakti times meant submitting to what is determined by one's karma. If things happen as we desire, it is the grace of God (Hari-krupa). If things don't happen as we desire, it is the will of God (Hari-ichha). Hari is another name for Vishnu. It is also another word for monkey. And monkey is a metaphor for the restless human mind.

Western scholars using Western religious frameworks and the atheistic contempt for religions, often reduce Hindu devotion (bhakti) to some kind of feudalism with God presiding as master. They ignore the strong component of affection and love in the relationship, like a parent's for a child (vatsalya-bhav), like a lover for their beloved (madhurya-bhav), like a friend for a companion (sakha-bhav). Bhakti is essentially the construction of an emotional highway connecting the devotee to the divine. God is not always in a position of power: he can also be the playful child, the gullible hermit, the mischievous monkey; which enables the devotee to take on the role of a parent, or a friend. Hanuman can be at once awesome (adbhuta) and silly, displaying monkey qualities (kapitva). The latter part is missing in most non-Hindu religions.

If one looks at the verse carefully, one realizes that the deity works for the devotee. The devotee submits and then the deity works to enable the happiness and security of the devotee. And so, in this verse, the protection is a kind of spiritual hug from God that comforts the frightened and lost devotee. The emotional aspect of the divine elevates the stature of the otherwise rustic guardian and fertility gods of the village. From material, he becomes spiritual, transcendent. He makes the devotee feel that he matters, for there is someone celestial watching out for him, even if fellow humans do not. Thus the devotee is granted meaning.

Chaupai 23: Three Worlds

आपन तेज
सम्हारो आपै ।
तीनों लोक
हाँक तें काँपै ॥

Aapan tej
samharo aapai.
Teenhon lok
hank te kanpai.

Your glory
You alone can contain.
The three worlds
Tremble when you roar.

This verse refers to the glory of Hanuman manifesting as his radiance and his roar. No one can contain his radiance and no one can withstand his roar. Yet, despite this great power, Hanuman does not seek to dominate the three worlds, which distinguishes him from other powerful people. His power is balanced by his immersion in the idea of Ram.

The quest for power (siddhi) from the divine is the central theme of Tantra, while the quest for immersion in the divine (samadhi) is the central theme of Vedanta. These two arms of Hinduism complement each other. In Tantra, the world is power (shakti); in Vedanta, the world is delusion (maya). Tantra seeks control over nature; Vedanta seeks transcendence. Tantra binds us to the earth and the world below, while Vedanta elevates from the earth to the world above. Hanuman's tales span the dark regions below the earth to the bright regions above the sky. In other words, he features across Tantrik as well as the Vedantic landscapes, adored by followers of Tantra and Vedanta, who would otherwise be rivals. Between these two antagonistic worlds is the world of Bhakti, the emotional highway between devotee and deity, the self and the other.

The concept of three worlds is found in the Vedas and the Puranas, but is very different in both. In the Vedas, the three worlds are the earth, the sky and the atmosphere in between. Indra separates the earth and sky and creates the three worlds. His younger brother, Vishnu, can traverse it in three steps and is hence known as Trivikrama, conqueror of the three worlds. The Vedic gods are classified as those who live on earth (fire, for example), those who live in the sky (the sun, for example) and those who live in between (wind, for example).

In the Puranas, on the other hand, the three worlds refer to earth, the celestial regions (Swarga), home to the devas, and the nether regions (Patala), home to nagas and asuras. Initially, there was not anything negative about the nether world. The two were just different. But gradually, perhaps under the influence of Christianity, or Islam, as society became increasingly linear in its worldview, the devas came to be seen as forces of good, while the asuras came to be seen as forces of evil. Devas started being associated with Vedanta, while asuras were linked with Tantra.

Patala was equated with hell (Naraka) and Swarga with heaven.

There are two Adbhut Ramayanas, both written roughly 500 years ago, one in Assamese and one in Sankrit, which reveal the different ways in which Patala was seen. In both, Hanuman plays an important role.

In the Assamese Adbhut Ramayana, Hanuman enters the kingdom of serpents, Naga-loka, located under the earth, to rescue Luv and Kush, abducted by Vasuki, king of serpents, on the instructions of Sita, who misses her children. The story comes from a local retelling of the final chapter of the Ramayana where gossip in the streets of Ayodhya about Sita's relationship with Ravana leads to Ram casting her away in the forest while she is pregnant, an episode that bothers most devotees of Ram. Sita raises her two children, the twins Luv and Kush, on her own and lets them go back to their father, but refuses to return to Ayodhya herself, choosing instead to descend into the earth, for she is the daughter of the earth. But then she misses her children and wants Vasuki to bring them from Bhu-loka to Naga-loka. In the war that follows, a compromise is reached. The children return to earth and Sita promises to visit them and their father in secret. Thus the royal family of Ayodhya is reconciled thanks to Hanuman.

The idea of Hanuman watching over Sita and her children when she was in the forest is a theme found in many folk retellings of the final chapter of the Ramayana. He takes the form of a monkey and plays with Luv and Kush, watching over them, providing them food and revealing to them the secrets of the forest. Only Sita knows what Hanuman is up to.

In the Sanskrit Adbhut Ramayana, also based on regional stories from the eastern part of India that is renowned for its

Tantra followers, Hanuman goes to Patala where he encounters not nagas, but asuras, demons and ghouls who worship Kali, perform human sacrifices and practice sorcery.

In this work, Ravana invokes his sorcerer brother, Mahiravana, who abducts Ram and Lakshman and takes them to Patala to offer them as sacrifices to Kali or Bhairavi. In the previous verses, we learnt of Hanuman as a doorkeeper and a guardian and provider of shelter. In the Adbhuta Ramayana, Hanuman uses his tail to create a fortress in which Ram and Lakshman can be safe. He lets no one in. Still, Mahiravana is able to outwit him and abduct the two brothers and take them to a place below the earth where there is no sun or wind.

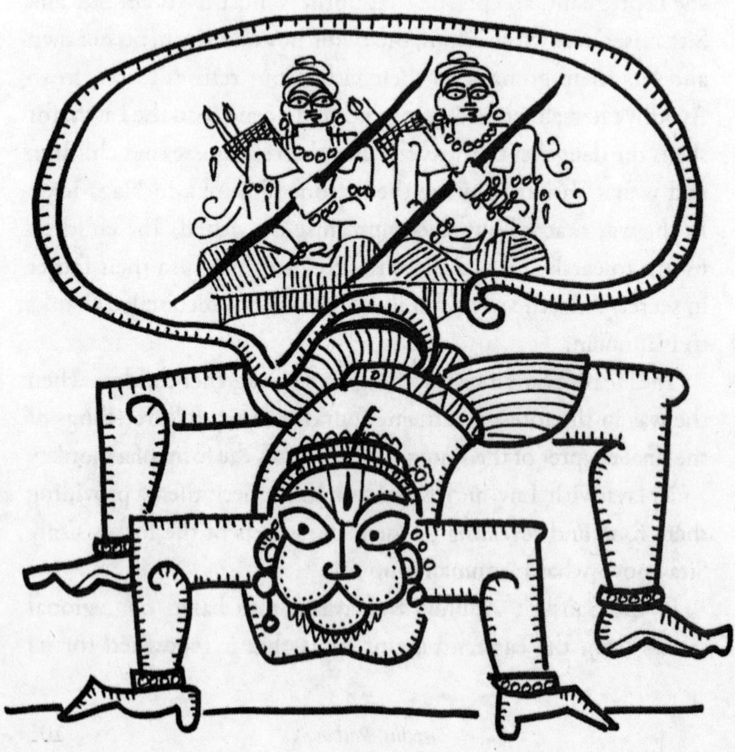

At the entrance of Patala, Hanuman meets a doorkeeper, who is part monkey and part fish, who refuses to let him in. In the duel that follows, Hanuman realizes he has met his match. 'Who are you?' he asks. The doorkeeper identifies himself as the son of Hanuman. How is that possible, wonders Hanuman, for he is a celibate ascetic. The warrior explains that he was born when a fish in the sea consumed a drop of Hanuman's sweat that fell as he was flying across to Lanka. When Hanuman reveals his identity, his son bows to him, and lets him pass, revealing to him the many secrets of the subterranean region.

Hanuman enters Patala, defeats the demons and ghouls there and outwits Mahiravana who he eventually beheads, thus pleasing Kali and asking her to never demand human sacrifice again. Kali places the condition that Hanuman should serve her, after Ram leaves the earth. Hanuman agrees.

In one of the many plots of this story, Hanuman has to simultaneously extinguish five lamps located in five different directions to kill Mahiravana's son, Ahiravana, which he is able to accomplish by sprouting four extra heads—that of an eagle, horse, lion and wild boar. This form of Hanuman with five heads transforms him from a god who is part of Ram's entourage, to an independent god in his own right. In other words, this story transforms Hanuman from being dependent on Ram to becoming dependable for Ram, from devata to bhagavan, from Ram-das to Maha-bali, from karya-karta to karta, for he takes initiative and decisions on his own, and not instructions from Ram.

The Hanuman who went to Patala, or Patali Hanuman, is a special form of Hanuman invoked for protection from sorcery. Patali Hanuman's temples are often located close to temples of the Goddess. Near Indore in Madhya Pradesh there is a temple to Ulte (upside down) Hanuman, for it is believed that everything in Patala is upside down.

Chaupai 24: Frightens Away Ghosts

भूत पिसाच
निकट नहिं आवै ।
महाबीर
जब नाम सुनावै ॥

Bhoot pisaach
nikat nahin aavai.
Mahabir
jab naam sunavae.

Ghosts and ghouls
don't come near.
Hanuman's name
when they hear.

This is undoubtedly the most popular verse of the Hanuman Chalisa, chanted when one is frightened and restless. It is said to drive away ghosts and spirits, or at least give one the strength to face what we believe to be ghosts and spirits.

Until the rise of modern psychology and medicine, around the world, mental disorders were seen as the work of ghosts and spirits. And so, this hymn has as much to do with the paranormal as it has to do psychiatry. Those who believe in ghosts believe that this hymn drives ghosts away. Those who see ghosts as merely external manifestations of internal fears believe this hymn helps strengthen the mind to overcome internal fears. It is not by accident that the word for ghost, 'bhoot', also means the past.

The idea of ghosts is different in different cultures. In Greek mythology, a ghost is believed to be the aspect of a living person that outlives death. Ghosts need to travel from the land of the living to the land of the dead, across the River Styx. Those who are unable to make the journey make life miserable for the living with their mourning, wailing and rage at their unfulfilled desires. In Christian mythology, the word soul is used instead of ghost. After death, souls wait in purgatory for Final Judgement. Then, depending on the deeds of their life, God takes them to Heaven or casts them in Hell. Some escape purgatory and haunt earth and have to be driven away using God's name.

In Hindu mythology, the River Vaitarni separates the land of the living from the land of the dead and souls move both ways continuously, as Hindus believe in multiple lives. The beings in the land of the dead are called pitrs, or ancestors. The dead who are trapped in the land of the living turn into pretas, or ghosts, colloquially known as bhoot. They torment the living. They hunger for a proper death ritual and rebirth. Some pretas refuse to become pitr as they have unfulfilled wishes that they need the living to assure them will be fulfilled. Other pretas refuse to become pitr as they are consumed by a sense of injustice, having died in a violent death, for instance, and so they yearn for justice. Many pretas are simply those who died while travelling and whose relatives do not know of their death and so have not conducted suitable rites for their passage across the Vaitarni.

Pisachas, or vetals, are different from bhoot and pret. They are one of the many sets of children fathered by Kashyapa, son of Brahma, such as the deva, asura, rakshasa, yaksha, naga, garuda, gandharva, apsara, and kinnar. They prefer night to day. They hang from solitary trees and prefer crematoriums. They speak a secret language called Paisachi. They enchant travellers in the forest and eat them alive, enjoying their flesh and their fear. They can have sex with a living creature that is asleep and such a person wakes up mad; this is why sex with a sleeping person is described as Paisachi maithuna.

Images of Shiva and Hanuman are kept in Hindu crematoriums to protect the living from pretas and pisachas. In folklore, Hanuman's father, either Kesari or Vayu, had another wife who was a cat and she gave birth to Preta-raja, lord of ghosts, who some identify with Yama. As a half-brother of Preta-raja, Hanuman is invoked to get rid of negative and malevolent forces that can afflict people tormented by ghosts and ghouls. One temple where this idea of exorcism is the central theme is the Mehendipur temple of Balaji Hanuman in Rajasthan.

There are also folktales where a wandering preta or pisacha can be captured by a sorcerer and made to do his bidding. So even the pretas and pisachas who encountered Hanuman's power during his adventures in Patala worship Patali Hanuman to protect them from such sorcerers. Hanuman, thus, protects the living from the dead and the dead from such sorcerers.

In Tantrik lore, Chamunda is seen in crematoriums riding pretas with an entourage of pisachas. She is worshipped in this form at Betal-Deul in Bhubaneswar, Odisha. This ghastly site can drive people insane unless they seek the protection of Shiva and Hanuman.

This verse refers to chanting the name of Hanuman as protection from these external, malevolent forces. Chanting the name of the divine (nam-jap) became a very popular means to invoke the divine in the Bhakti period. In Vedic times, in order to invoke the gods Brahmins had to know Sanskrit hymns, their complex pronunciations and meaning, and chant them at appropriate times, with appropriate gestures and rituals. But with time, and the rise of Bhakti, people rejected the complex ways of priests and came to believe that faith alone could invoke the divine. Faith was expressed by simply concentrating on the deity. And this was facilitated by chanting their name, or a set of names, or a sound (bija mantra) that represented the deity.

Many people believe in the concept of aura or energy fields that surrounds all things. Everyone has an inherent aura but it depletes over time. It can be replenished from outside as well as inside. Humans especially can invoke it from within—through prayer and faith. Many are unable to regenerate their own auras and so need the help of external instruments, such as talismans, crystals, gemstones, beads and coloured cloth. Then there are humans who feed on other people's auras like predators feed on prey. To create a force field around oneself from such predators, to combat the drain of energy created by social trauma, psychological afflictions and paranormal phenomena, and to restore health and harmony, one can invoke positive energies simply by chanting Hanuman's name.

Chaupai 25: Takes Away Ailments

नासै रोग
हरै सब पीरा ।
जपत निरंतर
हनुमत बीरा ॥

Nase rog
harae sab peera.
Japat nirantar
Hanumat Beera.

All diseases
and pain vanish.
When one continuously
chants your name.

If the previous chaupai focussed on mental health and paranormal phenomena, this chaupai focuses on physical health. Hanuman, the mighty warrior and patron god of bodybuilders and wrestlers, is seen as an agent of good health, one who gets rid of diseases and pain.

Hanuman is closely associated with Ayurveda, the traditional Indian system of health and healing, according to which health is the outcome of harmony between water (kapha), fire (pitta) and wind (vata) in the body. Disharmony results in disease. Hanuman, son of the wind, helps in maintaining harmony.

Hanuman is closely associated with yoga, which the yoga sutra defines as de-crumpling the mind crumpled by hunger, insecurity and imagination. Doctors have always known that many physical ailments such as insomnia, skin rashes, allergies, asthma, hypertension and indigestion are actually psychosomatic—having their origins in the mind—and so calming the restless and frightened mind, by a rhythmic, repetitive activity, like chanting God's name, arrests unnecessary thoughts and resolves many health issues too.

This de-crumpling of the mind can be achieved by various modulations of breath and body postures. Hanuman is associated with pranayama, breathing exercises that ensure proper oxygenation of the blood and also relieve mental stress. He is also associated with asanas, physical postures invented by Hanuman as he jumped from tree to tree and mimicked various forest creatures. Asanas strengthen the joints, the muscles and the ligaments of the body, and when done in alignment with breath, these postures affect the oxygenation of blood and can calm the restless mind.

Hanuman also designed the Surya-namaskar (sun salutation) to venerate his guru, the sun god. He designed the physical discipline of Malkhamb, popular in Maharashtra, wherein boys and girls go up and down a pole, like a monkey on a tree, to improve their flexibility and agility. The act of chanting plays an important role in calming the restless and tumultuous mind and releases body-harming hormones and chemicals.

Hanuman's association with Sanjivani has linked him to all herbs that cure the most lethal of ailments. The Dronagiri mountain that he brought from the Himalayas to Lanka to save

Lakshman from near death is said to be the source of various medicinal herbs. Offerings to Hanuman include preparations of urad dal, til and butter that are rich in protein and fat, necessary for fighting disease, firing up the metabolism and lubricating the joints. The poisonous Arka leaves and flowers he is offered at temples are a reminder of how he is the embodiment of all antidotes, and can withstand the fiercest of toxins.

Chaupai 26: Aligning with the Divine

संकट तें
हनुमान छुड़ावै ।
मन क्रम बचन
ध्यान जो लावै ॥

Sankat te
Hanuman chudavae.
Man, kram, vachan
dhyan jo lavai.

Problems
Hanuman takes away.
When the heart, action and word
are fixed on him.

In this verse, we discover how we can get the grace of Hanuman: he will remove our problems provided we concentrate on him, aligning mind (man), action (karam) and speech (vachan).

The key word here is dhyan. It means focus or concentration

and is a kind of mental exercise that is part of the yogic tradition. This word became cha'an in China, and zen in Japan, as Buddhism spread to the Orient.

Concentration may have been a part of Vedic rituals, however it was the Buddha who, nearly 2,500 years ago, transformed it into a technique to awaken the mind so that one could witness the truth about the world, that it is impermanent and our desire for it is the cause of our suffering. By the Bhakti era, 500 years ago, concentration had become a tool to invoke Hanuman to solve one's problems—whether psychological (stress, fear, ghosts), physical (ailments, pain), or social (danger, misfortune)—and take away our suffering (sankat). Sankat Mochan, or the remover of problems, is a popular form of Hanuman; it is the name by which he is revered in the city of Varanasi.

While monastic orders are all about withdrawing inwards into the mind by shutting the senses, Hinduism functions from the premise that not all humans can go through life simply by withdrawing inwards; they need external support. This consideration for diversity, and avoidance of homogeneity, is a hallmark of Hinduism.

The average human being needs a god out there who listens and cares. We realize this need clearly when we trace the history of Buddhism. As Buddhism spread, the concept of the Bodhisattva—who was very different from the Buddha—emerged. While the Buddha shut his eyes and trained his mind to concentrate on the truth, training others to do the same, the Bodhisattva kept his eyes and ears open to hear the suffering of the people, and stretched out his hand to help them. The suffering concentrated on the saviour Bodhisattva, rather than the teacher Buddha. The Theravada (original school) Buddhists, who preferred focussing on the Buddha's way, broke away from Maha-yana (elevated school) Buddhists, who encouraged worship of the Bodhisattva.

In Hinduism, there was no such breakup between the intellectual and the popular. The Gurus of Vedanta who wrote in Sanskrit and discussed complex theories of truth—such as Shankara, Ramanuja, Ramananda, Madhwa, Vallaha—all saw the value of devotion as complementing the intellectual and meditative approach. At one level they spoke of abstract Vedic ideas; this was Nigama parampara. Simultaneously, they spoke of the worship of various Hindu deities, Hanuman included; this was Agama parampara.

Hanuman becomes a form through which a devotee in stress can regain hope and strength. The act of praying to him, concentrating on him, gives strength—strength to be patient until fortune arrives, and strength to face misfortune when it arrives. Hinduism turned the act of prayer into simultaneously an external theistic practice (invoking God) and yogic practice (de-crumpling the mind crumpled by stress).

The word dhayan in this verse reveals an implicit understanding of yoga, the de-crumpling of the crumpled mind through restraint (yama), discipline (niyama), breathing (pranayama), postures (asana), withdrawal (pratyahara), concentration (dhayan), awareness (dharana) and immersion (samadhi).

Yoga also means alignment. By asking the devotee to align his concentration on Hanuman in mind, action and word, there is an implicit reference to Sankhya (Hindu metaphysics) that forms the canvas on which yoga is based. In Sankhya the world is divided into soul (dehi, or purusha) and body (deha, or prakriti). The body in turn is constituted by elements (mahabhutas), sense organs (gyan-indriyas), action organs (karma-indriyas), the heart (chitta), intelligence (buddhi), imagination (manas), memory (smara) and ego (aham). Problems arise when there is misalignment between what we think, what we do, and what we say—when we are forced to repress our feelings and pretend. Hanuman grants us the strength to cope with these everyday issues.

Yoga is also the process by which we discover the divine within us; bhoga is the indulgence of desire that seeks to ignore the truth of our body, our mind and our world. Yoga helps us place bhoga in perspective, recognize that pleasure is temporary, addictive and delusion-inducing, and not let desire sweep away all good sense. Hanuman is a yogi but not a bhogi. He has full perspective on the nature of desire, and desires nothing. We are bhogis, but not yogis. We seek his help in giving us the mental faculties we lack, and taking away the mental afflictions we suffer from.

Chaupai 27: Serving the Hermit-King

सब पर राम
तपस्वी राजा ।
तिन के काज
सकल तुम साजा ॥

Sab par Ram
tapasvee raja.
Tin ke kaj
sakal tum saja.

Ram who rules over all
Is the hermit-king.
All those tough tasks
You accomplish them easily.

The Chalisa gently makes its way from the external to the internal, from conversations on material success to psychological and physical well-being, to the idea of yoga, and the connection between a living creature and the divine. In the verse, all of us are described as the subjects of the hermit-king Ram, whose tasks are executed by Hanuman.

At one level, this verse establishes the relationship of Ram and Hanuman. Ram is the karta, the responsible leader, and Hanuman is the karya-karta, the obedient and effective follower. At another level, we are made to feel that it is Hanuman who enables Ram's rule, and so prayers to him are worthwhile, for one who makes the life of the king so easy can surely make the life of his subjects easy too.

This division between the grand but passive divine and the accessible and active divine is a common theme in many theistic schools around the world. In Christianity, even Zoroastrianism, there are archangels who carry out the will of God. In medieval India, the common folk rarely saw the king. They saw bureaucrats and soldiers fulfil the king's will. This is why worshippers of Shiva invoked Nandi, devotees of Vishnu invoked Garuda, and devotees of Ram invoked Hanuman.

Ram is the hermit-king because he desires neither kingship nor the fruits of kingship, these are his duties as the eldest son of the royal family. For him kingship is a role; he is not nourished by or dependent on the power that comes with the crown, which is why it is very easy for him to give it up. When he is asked to let his half-brother Bharat be king, he gives up his claim to the crown without regret or remorse. He is as happy in the forest as he is in the palace.

Both Ram and Hanuman are as happy in the forest as they are in Ayodhya, but Ram is obliged to be in Ayodhya because of his duty, while Hanuman gives up the forest out of love for Ram. Does that make Hanuman superior to Ram? One wonders. Thus one is cleverly drawn into the Vaishnava-Shaiva conflict that was prevalent in Varanasi at the time the Hanuman Chalisa was written. Ram, who is a Vishnu avatar, is burdened by kingship, and Hanuman, who is a Shiva avatar, helps Vishnu bear the burden with ease.

Hanuman's love for Ram is different from the romantic love of Sita for Ram, or Ram for Sita. Hanuman's love for Ram is the love of a devotee for a deity, of a seeker for a guru, of a student for a teacher, for the latter enables the former to transform himself, rise above his limitations. In other words, his mind expands: he moves from being dependent on the world to being independent of the world, and yet dependable *for* the world.

In medieval India, kings started identifying themselves as Ram, or descendants of Ram. They expected their followers to be like Hanuman, Sugriv and the obedient monkey army (vanar-sena). And so we find a large number of temples dedicated to Hanuman built by kings of the Vijayanagar and Maratha empires. They were inspired by acharyas such as Madhwa and Ramdas, who made Hanuman serving Ram and Bhima serving Yudhishitra, who in turn served Krishna, their models.

Love in political spaces is often described as standing by the beloved loyally no matter what and doing things for them without expecting anything in return. This logic is self-serving and does not see the larger narrative. For by this logic, Kumbhakarna's love for Ravana is no different from Hanuman's love for Ram.

Many loyal followers insist they are Hanuman, doing what their leaders tell them to do, thus implying that their leaders are Ram when, in fact, they are simply Kumbhakarnas who are following Ravana. The difference between Ram and Ravana is that Ram is a hermit-king. Ram desires nothing, least of all dominating people and establishing territory. He is content with himself. He does not even seek, or need, Hanuman's love. Ram is king by social obligation, not ambition, unlike Ravana. Ayodhya needs Ram; Ram does not need Ayodhya. By contrast, Ravana needs Lanka and the unconditional control over the rakshasas to feel powerful. For him, disobedience and disloyalty are indicators of a lack of love. Hence, he kicks Vibhishan out of the house and when Kumbhakarna dies, he blames Ram, refusing to see his own role in the unnecessary war.

Ravana is consumed by his ego, and so does not see the hurt he causes. All he sees is the hurt caused to him by others who do not obey him or who are not loyal to him. He sees Ram as the enemy, even though it is he who has captured Sita and kept her in Lanka against her consent. His craving for power and control reveals how hungry and frightened he is. He is no Ram. Ravana 'consumes' those who love him. Ram 'nourishes' those who love him. In serving Ram dutifully, Hanuman nourishes himself. He moves from being va-nara, less than human, to being Nara-ayana, refuge for humans.

Chaupai 28: Chariot of Desire

और मनोरथ
जो कोई लावै ।
सोई अमित
जीवन फल पावै ॥

**Aur manorath
jo koi lavai.
Sohi amit
jeevan phal pavai.**

*Any wish
one comes with.
Endless
fulfilment he receives.*

In this verse, wishes are described as 'mano-rath', the chariots of the mind, that propel our actions, and hence our life.

While Buddha said desire is suffering, and established monasteries, Hinduism advocated dharma, doing one's social role. The former disrupted social structure, the latter maintained social structure. Buddhist shrines (chaityas) were centres of silence and discipline, and introspective art. By contrast, Hindu temples (mandir) were centres of song and dance and food and celebratory art; the walls had images of beautiful women adorning themselves as men went about doing their duties.

When Buddhism waned, many Buddhist ideas expressed themselves in Hindu form: Hindu monasticism became a dominant force, challenging Hindu worldliness. The hermit sought liberation (moksha) from the world, while the householder spoke of social obligations (dharma) that sustained the world. Shiva, the hermit god was patron of the mathas (monasteries) where ash-smeared ascetics focussed on burning their desires just as Shiva had set aflame Kama, the god of desire. Vishnu, the householder god, was enshrined in grand temples that had separate sections such for food (bhoga-mandapa) and theatrical performances (natya-mandapa). How does one balance between moksha and dharma? This was done through the Goddess.

Every human being was seen as existing within an ecosystem of others. The relationships between humans were governed by desire and action. From desire came all the mental modifications: yearning, attachment, greed, pride, jealousy, frustration, rage; the source of all problems. Action, however, sustained the social fabric. The Goddess demanded focus on action and detachment from desire. In other words, plant the seed, do not desire the fruit. When put in a social context, this means working to satisfy other people's hunger and taking away other people's fear; striving hard to outgrow, rather than indulge, one's own hunger and fear.

And so the Goddess turns Shiva the hermit into Shankara the householder and gets him to descend from his mountaintop abode of Kailasa to the city of Kashi in the plains. Likewise, the Goddess becomes Lakshmi and Saraswati, and asks Vishnu to serve as her guardian. Brahma and his sons, be it the devas or asuras, nagas or yakshas, embody the other or those who are so focussed on their own hunger and fear that they are uninterested in the hunger and fear of the others. Hanuman, a student of the Goddess, on the other hand, focuses on satisfying the desires of others and seeking nothing for himself.

Hindu rituals are designed around this principle. Whether it was a Vedic yagna, or a later day puja at a temple, the yajaman makes offerings to a god and hopes to get something in return. Thus his desire is regulated: he does not just ask, or grab, he is made to first give something to the deity. He can give a gift (flowers, food, incense), or even words of praise (bhajan), or simply the gift of attention (darshan, dhayan). Then we pray the deity reciprocates. We have control over what we offer, how we offer it, when and where and to whom we offer it, but no control on what we receive, or don't receive. What we get is a function of whether the deity is pleased or not, and whether the deity is willing or not, or if the deity feels obliged or not. We have to accept what we get with grace and be at peace with what we don't get. So it is with the deity, so it is in life.

The chariot of desire is not the only force that governs the world. There is also karma, the cycle of actions and reactions. We may or may not get what we desire, but we certainly get what we deserve, based on the reactions of the past, and the actions of the present. Hanuman ensures we get what we should, and he ensures we have the strength to cope with what we don't get. That strength to enjoy what we get and be at peace with what we don't get is the eternal (amit, or amrit) fruit (phal) promised in this verse.

Chaupai 29: Four Eras

चारों जुग
परताप तुम्हारा ।
है परसिद्ध
जगत उजियारा ।

Chaaron jug
partap tumhara.
Hai persidh
jagat ujiyara.

Across four eras
Spans your glory.
Your fame
radiates through the world.

As mentioned earlier, Hindus believe that the world goes through cycles of birth and death, just as all living creatures go through cycles of birth of death. The 'world' here refers more to human culture, an organization or a system, rather than nature.

The lifespan of a world is called kalpa. It has four quarters (yuga, or jug, referred to in this verse): childhood, youth, maturity and old age known as Krita, Treta, Dvapara, and Kali, respectively. Ram lives in the Treta, hence he is called Treta ke Thakur. Krishna lives in the Dvapara, hence the name Dvapara ke Thakur. Hanuman lives across the four ages, hence he is also called Chiranjivi, the immortal one.

As Ram dies and returns to Vaikuntha at the end of the Treta yuga and Hanuman outlives him, greater emphasis is placed on the worship of Hanuman. People believe he still wanders the earth, and seek him out. There are legends that describe him living in the Himalayan region in a valley where there is a banana (kadali) grove (vana). During ritual readings of the Ramayana, a seat is placed specially for Hanuman, so that when he comes he has a place to sit and enjoy what he enjoys most—the story of his beloved Ram. Stories, and even photos, of his sightings are not uncommon. Some say he is the legendary Yeti or Big Foot of the mountains. For the believer, this is true; for the sceptic, it is simply the power of faith.

Since he is immortal, Hanuman plays an important role in both the Ramayana and the Mahabharata. In the Ramayana, he serves one avatar of Vishnu (Ram), and in the Mahabharata he helps another avatar of Vishnu (Krishna) enlighten the Pandava princes. He teaches the arrogant Bhima humility by taking the form of an old monkey and asking the mighty prince to lift his tail. A similar encounter takes place between Hanuman and Arjuna.

When Arjuna wonders why Ram did not build a bridge of arrows across the sea to Lanka, Hanuman, again in the form of an old monkey, replies saying such a bridge would not have been able to bear the weight of the monkey army. Arjuna tries to disprove this by building a bridge across a river using his own arrows, but the bridge breaks as soon as Hanuman steps on it. Then Krishna advises Arjuna to chant Ram's name while shooting his arrows. This time the bridge does not break. Arjuna realizes that it is not just the material strength of arrows, or stones, that creates the bridge; it is also the grace of Ram's name.

A humbled Arjuna asks Hanuman to sit atop his chariot during the war against the Kauravas. Arjuna declares his flag to be kapi-dhvaja, as it displays the image of a monkey, a symbol of the restless mind which can transform into Hanuman when it has faith in Ram.

Chaupai 30: In China

साधु संत
के तुम रखवारे ।
असुर निकंदन
राम दुलारे ॥

Sadhu sant
ke tum rakhware.
Asur nikandan
Ram dulhare.

Sages and saints
are protected by you.
You who destroy demons
are much loved by Ram.

Over 1,500 years ago, many pilgrims from China came to India seeking original Buddhist manuscripts. During their travels here they came upon stories of Hanuman which they carried back with them. These stories mingled with ancient Taoist stories of an incredible white monkey who had miraculous strength and powers. And so, in Chinese literature we find a Chinese version of Hanuman, one who travels with a Chinese monk, Hsuan Tsang, in his perilous journey through the west (India). His name is Sun Wukong. And he does precisely what this verse states: protects sages and destroys demons. Coincidentally, the famous Chinese novel describing this monkey-king's feats was written in China around the same time the Hanuman Chalisa was written in India.

Born from a rock that was touched by the wind, Sun Wukong is incredibly strong and fast and had powers to change his form, just like Hanuman. Unlike Hanuman, he makes himself king of all the monkeys by displaying his incredible powers and strength.

In Sun Wukong's hand he has a special magical staff, much like Hanuman's mace, but while the monkey-king's staff is an important aspect of his personality and plays a key role in his adventures, Hanuman's mace has only symbolic value in Hindu iconography. It is entirely possible that originally Hanuman was shown holding the trunk or branch of a tree as a weapon which eventually metamorphosed into the mace (malla, or gada, in Sanskrit) used by bodybuilders and wrestlers.

Like Hanuman, the monkey-king did not know his strength; his unruly wild side needed to be contained. So in the Ramayana Hanuman was cursed to forget his powers until the time was right, while in the Chinese novel, after the Jade Emperor of Heaven was unable to stop him from consuming the Peaches of

Immortality, the heavenly Adi Buddha intervened, to humble him. The Buddha asked the arrogant monkey to find the edge of the world. Sun Wukong found it and boasted that he had made a mark on one of the five pillars that stand at the edge of the world. 'Is this the mark?' asked the Buddha, showing him one of his fingers. On seeing it, Sun Wukong realized that what he thought was the whole world was just the palm of the Buddha's hand.

The humbled monkey was given the task of helping Hsuan Tsang retrieve sacred Buddhist texts from the west in exchange for freedom. But to control this mischievous rake, the Bodhisattva Guanyin got Hsuan Tsang to trick the monkey-king into wearing a headband. The monk could constrict the headband, and the resulting headache would rein in the monkey-king whenever he got too unruly. This taming of the monkey theme is not found in the Ramayana. Hanuman voluntarily submits to Ram, and venerates his divinity. Ram neither seeks Hanuman's submission nor does he display his own divinity.

After many adventures, one of which involved defeating a demon who had abducted a princess and reuniting her with her beloved, the pilgrim returned to China, his mission successful, thanks to the help of the monkey-king. The monkey-king Sun Wukong was rewarded with Buddhahood and revered by all as the 'Victorious Fighting Buddha,' an important character in Chinese Buddhism.

Chaupai 31: Goddess and Tantra

अष्टसिद्धि
नौ निधि के दाता ।
अस बर दीन
जानकी माता ॥

Ashta-sidhi
nav-nidhi ke data.
As bar deen
Janki mata.

Eight powers
Nine treasures you bestow.
As per the wishes of
Janaka's daughter (Sita)

This verse explicitly elevates Sita to the level of Goddess and establishes her connection to Hanuman, revealing the influence of the Shakta school of Hinduism. Initially, Hanuman was linked to Vedic gods, then to Vishnu, then to Shiva, and finally to the Goddess. Here, Sita is presented not just as the wife of Ram, but also as the daughter of Janaka, himself a hermit-king. She is being addressed as mother, which is a title of respect as well as a term for the female divine. Sita blesses Hanuman that he can grant the seeker both siddhis and nidhis. Siddhis refer to powers that enable one to manipulate one's body and one's ecosystem and nidhis refer to secret treasures. Embodied, 'Siddhi' and 'Nidhi' can be seen as Tantrik forms of Saraswati and Lakshmi.

Hinduism has two branches—Vedanta, which is spiritual and mystical, focussing on the mind and soul, and Tantra, which is material and occult, focussing on the body and the world. The object of worship in Vedanta is the male form of the divine—Ram—while the object of worship in Tantra is the female form of the divine, so Sita.

Around 500 years ago, many Shakta Ramayanas were written that linked Sita to the Goddess. Here she is described as the wild Kali who voluntarily becomes the demure Gauri, embodiment of forest and field, enabling Ram's greatness. While Ram could kill the ten-headed Ravana, Sita secretly killed a thousand-headed brother of Ravana, a secret that Ram revealed to Lakshman. In these Tantrik tales, the Goddess enables God; without Shakti,

Shiva is a mere corpse (shava), and Ram would not be able to establish Ram-rajya. It is she who gives Hanuman the power to defeat demons and rescue her.

The various siddhis are the ability to reduce one's size (anima), expand one's size (mahima), make oneself heavy (garima), make oneself weightless (laghima), acquire anything from any space (prapti), satisfy any desire (prakamya), duplicate oneself (ishtva), and dominate all (vastva). Hanuman's many adventures reveal that he has access to this knowledge which is why he can change his size and shape, and fly. In one story, he asks the rakshasas to move his leg and they are unable to, for such is his strength.

The secret treasures have many names such as Mahapadma, Padma, Sankha, Makara, Kacchapa, Mukunda, Kunda, Nila and Kharva. Though Hanuman has access to so much power and wealth, he wants nothing because he is a yogi who has everything but wants nothing. This is why all the gods adore him. This is what makes him the chosen deity of many followers of Tantra.

Both Kali and Hanuman are part of the pantheon adored by the Nath-jogis, or Nath-yogis, who see Shiva as the Adi-guru, or teacher of teachers. These ascetics believe in celibacy and own no property, but are believed to have immense power (the siddhis) and access to many treasures (the nidhis). Their first teacher, Matsyendra-nath, was a fish who overheard a conversation between Shiva and Shakti and so became a human and a jogi. His student, Gorakh-nath, was created from cowdung ash.

In Nath folklore, if a yogi acquires power by resisting sex, then the yogini acquires power by seducing the yogi. This makes them antagonists. The yoginis live in an enchanted banana grove that turns all men into women. Only a yogi can resist the spell of these women and enter this enchanted grove. Matsyendra-nath was ensnared by the queen of these yoginis and had to be rescued by Gorakh-nath who entered this kingdom of women by disguising himself as one. When the women of this kingdom wanted children, they begged the Goddess to help. She sent Hanuman. Hanuman, however, being a brahmachari wondered how he could satisfy the wishes of these women and keep the word of the Goddess. Seeking a solution, he began to sing a song in praise of Ram. So powerful was the song, its words and its tune, and the voice of Hanuman, that all the women who heard this song became pregnant.

Historically, this branch of Hinduism originated about a thousand years ago, around the time when Hinduism became increasingly monastic and many monks chose to be wandering warriors, offering their services to local warlords and kings, but refusing to marry and settle down. They saw themselves as embodying the principle of the immortal Hanuman, who promised to help the world even after Ram returned to Vaikuntha.

Chaupai 32: Serving God

राम रसायन
तुम्हरे पासा ।
सदा रहो
रघुपति के दासा ॥

Ram rasayan
tumhare pasa.
Sada raho
Raghupati ke dasa.

Ram's chemistry
Is known to you.
May you forever be
Servant of the lord of the Raghu clan (Ram).

If there is one thing that Hanuman wants, it is to serve Ram.

One day, Hanuman asked Sita why she marked her forehead with a red dot. She told him that it was a sign of her love for Ram. Hanuman concluded that the colour red indicates the chemistry (rasayan) between devotee and deity. Hanuman wondered how much red colour he would need to indicate his love for Ram, since he was a mere monkey, and a servant, far lower in stature to Sita, the consort of Ram. He finally decided to colour his entire body with red powder, which is why Hanuman images are coloured red in temples dedicated to him, it is believed. Deities associated with the Goddess, such as Ganesha (her son) and Hanuman (her guard), are typically coloured red, a colour usually associated with the Goddess.

Hanuman used to serve Ram diligently, so much so that no one else had the pleasure of taking care of Ram's needs. Exasperated, one day Ram's brothers and Sita and other members of the Raghu clan decided to make a list of all of Ram's needs and divide the chores amongst them. Hanuman was left with nothing to do. Hanuman did not mind, after all, he realized that everyone needs the pleasure of taking care of Ram. But he was keen to do something for Ram. He noticed that the list did not have one task: snapping fingers when one yawns. The people of Ayodhya believed that if you did not snap your fingers while yawning, disease-causing spirits entered the body. Surely, the act of snapping fingers while Ram yawned could be outsourced to him, thought Hanuman. Better a monkey do this menial task than Ram himself, or anyone else in the family, for that matter. So Hanuman kept following Ram everywhere, to everyone's annoyance, carefully waiting for the moment Ram would yawn so that he could click his fingers. But at night, he could not enter

Ram's private chambers. He waited at the door, wondering how he would know when Ram yawned inside. Rather than wait for Ram to yawn, Hanuman thought of snapping his fingers continuously—that way, whenever Ram happened to yawn at night, he wouldn't miss it. Unfortunately, his plan had a disastrous impact—every time he snapped his fingers Ram would start yawning inside, so that his devotee's chores did not go waste. All night, Hanuman kept snapping his fingers, and Ram, instead of sleeping, kept yawning. When the reason for this was discovered, everyone laughed. They realized they could take Hanuman away from Ram, but not Ram away from Hanuman.

Stories such as these, popular in the oral tradition, seek to convey the deep bond of the relationship between Hanuman and Ram.

The idea of selflessly serving Ram who seeks the welfare of the world is often used by political leaders who want their followers to be like Hanuman, and serve their constituency. But such a parallel is dangerous. For it assumes that leaders are Ram and followers are Hanuman, by default.

Both leaders and followers work hard to project that they are indeed hermits, seeking no personal gain from their political powers. So they shun family, property, luxury and pleasure, and are seen in public wearing white or saffron clothing. They understand that the masses equate the superficial with the psychological.

We can see matter, not mind. We can see saffron costumes, not the yogic mind. We assume that those dressed in simple clothes, who shun wine, and sex, and non-vegetarian food, must be hermits. But these are assumptions, matters of faith.

Just as we can see clothes and not the mind, we can see wealth not power. A leader or follower may not care for wealth, but they often seek power. This hunger for power manifests in the desire to control people, dominate people, direct people and in territorial behaviour. This is seen in political parties as they fight for votes, and the power to control people through law enforcement. This is seen in spiritual organizations where the only decision-maker is the guru. This is seen in institutions that split after the charismatic 'hermit' founder-leader dies. This is seen in the constant yearning for social status and respect and media attention that many 'gurus' crave for, even as they give elaborate, hair-splitting arguments about how desire is different from ambition, and how their business and political activities are actually manifestations of dharma.

Power is Durga, who rides a lion. Durga is as seductive as

Lakshmi but far more insidious. Even those who seek Saraswati, scholars, experts and artists, and who insist they don't care for Lakshmi, eventually use their knowledge and skill and art to dominate, argue, direct, control and assert authority. These are all signs that the aham is thriving and the atma is eclipsed.

When the atma shines, we don't crave wealth, power or knowledge, as we are wealthy, powerful and knowledgeable, like Ram and Hanuman, we are happy in the palace as well as in the forest. When the atma shines, the other matters more than the self. And it is the other who decides who is a leader. Ram does not want to be the leader. Hanuman, however, wants to follow Ram. To realize this is to realize Ram's chemistry (rasayan).

Chaupai 33: Karma and Rebirth

तुम्हरे भजन
राम को पावै ।
जनम जनम के दुख
बिसरावै ॥

Tumhare bhajan
Ram ko pavai.
Janam-janam ke dukh
bisraavai.

Singing your praises
leads to Ram.
Sorrows accumulated over lifetimes
are hence forgotten.

In this verse, we learn that the benefit of adoring Hanuman is not to just get fruits in this life, but also to forget the sorrows of multiple lives, by finding Ram.

The idea of living multiple lives distinguishes the Indic faiths from Abrahamic faiths. In Hinduism, Buddhism and Jainism, we live multiple lives, whereas in Judaism, Christianity and Islam it is believed that we live only one life. In one-life cultures, we have one life to lead a perfect life; in multiple-life cultures, every life is an outcome of the ones that came before. In one-life cultures, the quest is to align oneself to the rules of God revealed through His messenger; in multiple-life cultures, the quest is to either stop the cycle of rebirths, or overpower the suffering that comes as a carry-over from each life. In one-life cultures, God is outside, watching us, loving us, judging us, as we live our one and only life; in multiple-life cultures, God is within, awaiting discovery patiently over multiple lives.

Karma means action. Karma also means the reaction to that action. Reactions to past actions create the circumstances that we encounter in our present life. Thus, when we face an opportunity, it is because of something we did in our past. And if we face a threat, it is also because of something we did in our past. How we react to an opportunity or a threat determines our present and our future. This is karma. This is very different from the popular understanding of karma as some kind of cosmic justice: as you sow, so you reap. And certainly not fatalism: your life is determined by past deeds. All the things that are not in our control are born of past actions. What is in our control is our current action. If the circumstances in our life are full of sorrow and misfortune, it indicates the terrible burden of past actions. Can we change the circumstances? No. What, then, can we do? This verse suggests we sing the song of Hanuman and find Ram.

The Ramayana reveals how bad things happen to the best of people for no fault of theirs, for reasons beyond their control. Ram is exiled to the forest, because of circumstances, because his father made a promise to his stepmother and because his stepmother was ambitious and because he, as a prince, was obliged to uphold a royal promise. It was not because he was a bad person or because anyone in his household hated him or wanted to hurt him. Likewise, Sita was doing a good deed: she was feeding a hungry man. But the results were bad: the hungry man turned out to be a demon who abducted her. Neither Ram nor Sita are ever angry or upset with the people around them, nor do they blame them for their misfortune. They suffer, without judging others, and find the inner strength to cope with the suffering. That inner strength comes from atma. Aham makes us blame.

In Hindu mythology, even God is not outside the realm of karma. In the Naradeya Purana, one hears the story of how once Narada asked Vishnu to give him Hari's face. Hari is a proper noun, the name of Vishnu, as well as a common noun, referring to a monkey. Narada wanted Vishnu's face to impress a princess but Vishnu gave him a monkey's face. When the princess saw Narada's new face she burst out laughing. When Narada discovered Vishnu's prank he cursed Vishnu that when he would descend on earth as Ram his success would depend on a monkey. So it came to pass that Ram needed Hanuman's help to find Sita and overpower Ravana. Curse is a mythological tool to explain karma. Even Vishnu, who is God, cannot escape the reaction to his actions.

Chaupai 34: Heavens

अंत काल
रघुबर पुर जाई ।
जहाँ जन्म
हरिभक्त कहाई ॥

Ant-kaal
Raghubar pur jayee.
Jahan janma
Hari-bhakt kahayee.

Eventually,
one goes to Ram's heaven.
Where for eternity,
one is known as Ram's devotee.

If the previous chaupai spoke of rebirth, this chaupai refers to immortal life in Ram's heaven. In the previous verse, singing the praises of Hanuman enables us to cope with this life's suffering born of actions in previous lifetimes. In this verse, the same activity grants us immortality and peace in the hereafter. Thus, these two verses deal with Hindu eschatology: death, rebirth and liberation. With this verse, we are now in the fourth quarter of the Hanuman Chalisa. Just as the verses in the first quarter deal with birth (of the deity) the verses in the final quarter deal with death (of the devotee).

In Hindu funeral rites, the dead body is cremated and the bones cast in a river. Thus fire and water claim the dead. Fire embodies the promise of immortality, while water embodies the promise of rebirth. Immortality and rebirth are the two options after death.

The Vedic Samhitas, over 3,000 years old, speak of an entity (prana, atma, jiva) outliving death. But the idea of rebirth fully develops only in the Upanishads, 2,500 years ago. The idea of Swarga, a temporary paradise of pleasures for those who have earned good merits in their life, and Vaikuntha, for those who want to break free from the cycle of rebirths, first appears in the Mahabharata roughly 2,000 years ago.

In the Puranas, one can be reborn in Swarga, where the fruits of good deeds are enjoyed or in Naraka, where one must suffer the consequences of bad deeds. The former is ruled by Indra, the king of devas and the latter is ruled by Yama, the king of pitr and preta. But stay in either location is temporary, as we learn in the Mahabharata. We can tumble down from Swarga when we use up our karmic equity, or rise up from Naraka when we exhaust our karmic debts.

In the Garuda Purana this is further elaborated with detailed descriptions of multiple hells to punish people who have committed different misdeeds. Chitragupta, assistant to Yama, maintains the book of accounts, determining if we are to go to heaven or hell, and if heaven, then which heaven and for how long, and if hell, then which hell and for how long. We keep going up and down over lifetimes depending on karmic baggage.

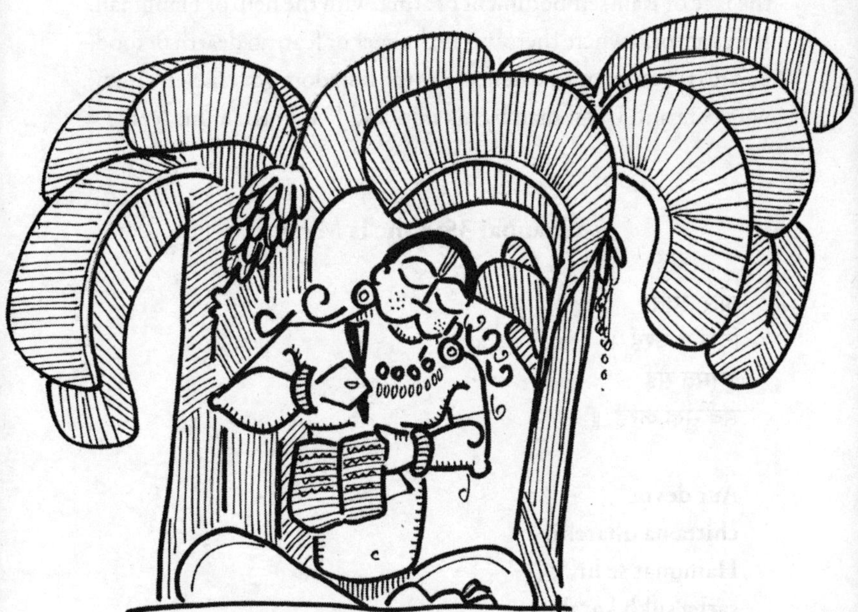

Freedom is breaking free from the karmic cycle, a balance sheet with no debts to repay. Then we go to the heaven of our choice and are there forever, experiencing neither death nor sorrow, gazing upon the deity of our choice. In the Vishnu Purana and Shiva Purana, there are heavens for Vishnu (Vaikuntha) and Shiva (Kailasa). Later, we find references to the heaven of Krishna (Go-loka), and the heaven of Ram (Saket, or Raghuvir pur). Still later, there are heavens for other gods which rise in popularity, like those of Ganesha (the sugarcane forest, ikshu-van) or that of Hanuman (the banana grove, kadali-van).

These structures gave form to abstract ideas like moksha to the common man. He realized that after death, there was the possibility of living in a world without any suffering, gazing upon the face of Ram, embodiment of atma, with the help of Hanuman. It was a world where there was no hunger or fear, no dearth of food, and no threat to our existence. It is the kingdom governed by Ram, with Sita and Lakshman by his side, and Hanuman at his feet.

Chaupai 35: One is Many

और देवता
चित्त न धरई ।
हनुमत सेई
सर्ब सुख करई ॥

Aur devta
chitta na dharehi.
Hanumat se hi
sarba sukh karahi.

All other deities
Do not connect.
Hanuman alone
Gives full delight.

This chaupai raises the question: is Hinduism polytheistic or monotheistic? For in this verse Hanuman is seen as the source of all happiness, so why bother with other deities. The other deities are not derided; they are just seen as not needed.

This question of monotheism and polytheism did not matter until the rise of European Orientalist studies in the 19th century. After having established their authority in the subcontinent, the Muslim rulers did not bother so much with this question, which is why Muslim communities and Hindu communities lived in relative harmony. But all this harmony was disrupted when European rulers kept wondering: what is true religion? In their view, polytheism was definely primitive, pagan, false, hence myth. Monotheism was true, especially one that saw Jesus as the son of God, not one that saw Muhammad as the last and final Prophet of God.

With the rise of postmodern studies in the late twentieth century, the politics underlying the word 'myth' was revealed and its association with falsehood and fiction discarded. Today, both polytheism and monotheism, like ideology and theology, are classified as different kinds of mythology, conceptual cultural truths, and distinguished from measurable and verifiable scientific truths. Of course, fundamentalists, and even many historians, academics and scientists, still cling to the old, outdated colonial meanings, and the binary of truth and falsehood.

Greek mythology is polytheistic while Abrahamic mythology is monotheistic. When the Roman Empire became Christian, polytheism was rejected as false religion. Hindu mythology has always been simultaneously polytheistic and monotheistic: the same God (spelt with capitalization) manifests as multiple gods (spelt without capitalization). In other words, the whole manifests as parts, and every part is an expression of the whole. The whole is limitless, and the part limited; the limitless whole is accessed through the limited part. This approach is unique to Hinduism, and remains unfathomable to most non-Hindus.

A word commonly used for Hinduism is kathenotheism, where one god is worshipped at a time, without disrespecting other gods, and that god is seen as representative of the limitless formless divine, or God. Hence the concept of ishta-devata, the One Being invoked, through whom the devotee accesses the cosmic soul (param-atma). Each deity is like a portal to the same divine entity, and each deity, despite its finite form, is the perfect embodiment of infinity.

In Hindu temples, Hanuman can be seen as an independent deity, or as a deity who is part of Ram's entourage, just as Ganesha or Murugan can be seen as independent deities, or a deity who is part of Shiva's family. A deity exists in an ecosystem of many deities and at the same time contains all deities within them.

Hanuman is one. But simultaneously, he is many. Through him, one accesses the hermit Shiva, the householder Vishnu, and the Goddess who embodies nature. He is a Vedic scholar as well as a potent Tantrik warrior. He is the embodiment of Bhakti. He is linked to literature and poetry, with song and music, with physical prowess as well as marital arts. He brings with him Durga (power), Saraswati (knowledge) and Lakshmi (prosperity).

For those uncomfortable with the idea of worshipping a celibate man, there are temples in India where Hanuman has a wife (in Hyderabad, for example), and also one where he wears a nose-ring to appear like the Goddess (in Ratanpur district, Chhattisgarh). So, says this verse, the most efficient way to worship infinity is through this one single deity.

Chaupai 36: Problem-Solver

संकट कटै
मिटै सब पीरा ।
जो सुमिरै
हनुमत बलबीरा ॥

Sankat kate
mite sab peera.
Jo sumirai
Hanumat Balbeera.

Problems cease
pain goes away.
When one remembers
Hanuman, the mighty hero.

This chaupai reiterates what Hanuman can do for us: remove problems and take away pain.

In the Ramayana, Hanuman solves Ram's problems. He finds Ram's missing wife, Sita, by leaping across the sea to the kingdom of Lanka. He saves Ram's injured brother, Lakshman, by carrying a mountain of herbs across the sky. He even saves Ram from being sacrificed by Mahiravana to Patala Bhairavi. If he can help God, surely he can help humanity. Perhaps this explains Hanuman's mass appeal.

Across India, at the start of roads that wind up hills and mountains, one frequently finds temples of Hanuman. People driving past in cars, buses and trucks, throw money at these temples, offerings to the great hero, to give them the strength to overcome the obstacle before them, and to keep out all obstacles from their path. A temple is also located at the end of the journey, on the other side of the mountain, where the travellers can thank Hanuman for protecting them from all potential danger.

At the frontier of most villages, and in most Hindu crematoriums, we find red-orange images of Hanuman, glistening with til oil, bedecked with Arka leaves and flowers, protecting the village from the wild, from diseases and demons, ghouls and ghosts. He embodies the positive side of masculinity (strength) but not the negative side (domination).

When Hanuman was flying over the ocean to Lanka, he defeated many monsters. But he did not stop to rest. Mount Mainaka rose from under the sea and requested Ram's messenger to sit on his slopes for a bit. Hanuman politely refused, for he had a task to complete. Thus Hanuman embodies selflessness, commitment, and integrity, the one who completes the most arduous task without resting. We yearn to have someone like Hanuman on our side. And to have him on our side, we need to invoke Ram in our hearts.

In folk retellings of the Ramayana, Ravana had locked up Shani, lord of Saturn; Mangal, the god of Mercury; and Preta-raja, or Mahakala, or Yama, lord of disease and death, under his throne. Hanuman released them and so Shani, Mangal, and Mahakala are in Hanuman's debt. If one prays to Hanuman on Saturday, the day associated with Saturn, then Shani, who delays things, does not assert his malevolent force. If one prays to Hanuman on Tuesday, the day associated with Mercury, then Mangal, who causes strife, does not assert his malevolent influence. And if one worships Hanuman at night, when Preta-raja rules, then disease and death, caused by negative energies and black magic, fail to act.

The Nawabs of Lucknow started the Bada Mangal festival, when Hanuman is worshipped with great fanfare every Tuesday in the summer month of Jyestha (May-June). This practice began after an image of Hanuman was found at a construction site. The story goes that the elephant carrying the deity to its new location stopped at one point and refused to budge. So the temple was built at the spot the elephant stopped. In this festival, local Hindus and Muslims participate, the latter providing water to the long queues of devotees who stand all through Tuesday night to see Bada Hanuman.

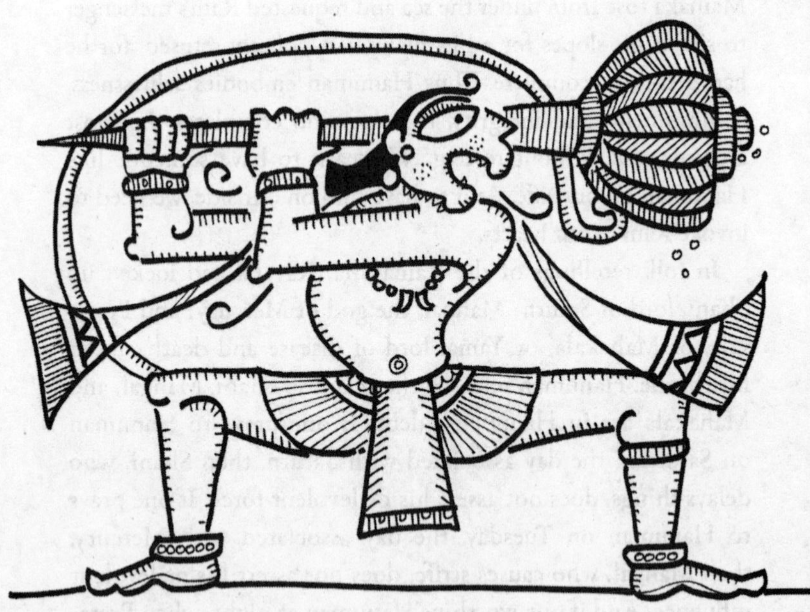

This verse reveals the most elemental form of Hanuman and resonates with humanity's most primitive past, when the things one wanted from divine forces were as basic as protection from dangers and cures from diseases. In the verses that follow, the higher needs of humanity are addressed, revealing Hanuman's versatility spanning from the most elemental to the most refined.

Chaupai 37: Guru and Gosain

जै जै जै
हनुमान गोसांई ।
कृपा करहु
गुरुदेव की नांई ॥

Jai Jai Jai
Hanuman Gosain.
Kripa karahu
gurudev ki nyahin.

Hail, Hail, Hail
Hanuman, lord of senses.
Be as kind
As the master.

In this chaupai, Hanuman is identified as gosain and is being asked to be as kind as his guru. So Hanuman, who in previous verses is being asked to solve material problems and relieve material pain, has here been sought to grant spiritual wisdom that will liberate us from material bondage.

The word gosain, or go-swami, is a Vedic metaphor. Ancient Hindus were aware that our understanding of the world begins with sensory awareness of the world around us. The five sensory organs (gyan-indriya) carry information to our mind (manas) and provoke emotions (chitta) and finally get our intellect (buddhi) to take decisions that are manifested through the five action organs (karma-indriya). Our intelligence is controlled by our ego (aham) and only a guru's guidance can help us break free from ego, and discover our soul (atma), our true self, that fears no death, is neither hungry nor insecure, and so can empathize with the other (para-jiva). The indriyas that continuously engaged with the world of sensory stimulations were metaphorically described as cows (go) grazing (chara) in a pasture. The one who had complete control over them was the go-swami, or gosain, master of the sense-cows. Gosain, thus, is a word for yogi commonly used by Vaishnavas and followers of Krishna. It was a title bestowed on students by their gurus.

If Hanuman is the gosain, who is Hanuman's teacher? Is it Surya, the sun god? Is it Ram, lord of the solar dynasty? Or is it Sita, the shakti of Ram? Maybe all three. This difference between guru and gosain reflects the difference between Jehovah and Jesus in Christianity, Allah and Prophet Muhammad in Islam, and the Buddha and Bodhisattva in Buddhism. In religious traditions around the world, there is invariably a medium between the spiritual and the material, between the deity and the devotee, between the transcendental and the phenomenal. That is the role being attributed to Hanuman, the gosain of the guru.

The Hanuman Chalisa was composed in times when the Mughals established their authority over the Gangetic plains.

The locals were very familiar with Islamic ideas of God and prophet, that had entered India five centuries prior to Tulsidas, that is, almost a thousand years ago from today. For local Hindus, the guru became the Hindu equivalent of the Islamic prophet, one who shows you the path to God. If Muslims had a paigambar for Allah, then Hindus had a Ram-doot for Ram. The similarity was convenient but deceptive. Convenient because it helped establish a connection between the two faiths and faciliate dialogue, in the spirit of plurality. And deceptive because Hindu ideas of God and teacher are very different from the Islamic idea of God and messenger.

God in Islam is formless and firmly located outside space and time, while his prophet has form and is located in history and geography. God in Hinduism is simultaneously formless and has form (Shiva, Vishnu), is simultaneously outside space and time (Vishnu) and inside history and geography (Ram and Krishna). The guru can be a real person located outside (Shankara-acharya, Ramanuja-acharya, Madhwa-acharya, Ramananda, Tulsidas), or a deity (Hanuman), or a voice inside our heart and head. In the Bhagavat Purana, the primal teacher (adi guru) Dattatreya describes nature as his guru. In Tantra, Shiva is Shakti's guru, Shakti is Shiva's guru. Thus in Hinduism, guru is gosain and gosain is guru, and guru is God and God is guru. The message and the messenger mingle and merge. Time, space and people are simultaneously outside and inside, literal and metaphorical, immanent and transcendent, objective and subjective, physical and psychological. This fluid aspect of Hinduism is most confounding to the outsider, as confounding as the Indian headshake.

Chaupai 38: Liberation

जो सत बार
पाठ कर कोई ।
छूटहि बंदि
महा सुख होई ॥

Jo sat bar
path kar koi.
Chhutehi bandhi
maha sukh hoyi.

Whoever a hundred times
recites this song.
Will be liberated
and very happy.

This chaupai states that chanting the Hanuman Chalisa a hundred times will grant us liberation. Hanuman will make this happen; it is the kindness he is asked to bestow upon us in the previous chaupai.

Happiness in Hinduism is of two types: material and spiritual. In material happiness, our desires are met. In spiritual happiness, we outgrow desire itself. The technique for the latter is known only to gurus, who reveal it to deserving students, the gosains, who master the techniques of yoga. But according to this verse, simply chanting the Hanuman Chalisa will invoke Hanuman who will grant us spiritual happiness. This outgrowing of desire is liberation.

Many people confuse the Hindu idea of liberation (mukti) with the Christian idea of salvation. In Christian mythology, humans are born in sin and can be saved from eternal damnation if they accept the love of Jesus Christ, the son of God, who takes upon himself the sins of the world. This is salvation. In Hindu mythology, humans are born in debt and incur more debt by indulging desires. Liberation happens when we repay this debt, and incur no more debts.

In Vedic times, the purpose of a yagna was simply to invoke deities for the sake of material happiness. But then the Buddha came along and declared this desire for material happiness as the root of all misery. He encouraged people to become monks. As more and more chose the monastic life over marriage, social structure was threatened. So the Dharma-shastras came to be written, and the idea of debt was elaborated upon. It was argued that liberation could not happen unless debts were repaid to the ancestors (pitr): they gave us life and were now in the land of the dead patiently waiting for their descendents to facilitate their return to the land of the living. Stories were told of forest hermits tormented by visions of suffering ancestors demanding they marry and produce children. Liberation could only follow the fulfilment of worldly obligations. In other words, after retirement!

Later, in the Bhagavad Gita, we find the idea that one does not have to renounce the world, or wait for retirement, to be liberated. We can be liberated while living the life of a householder, if we do our duties, without any expectations. This idea of one who is liberated while being a productive member of society is embodied in the idea of Ram. He is engaged with society, yet free. Chanting the Hanuman Chalisa, we are told, will give us the strength to fulfil our duties and so repay our debts, and at the same time, overcome our desires and prevent incurring new debts.

If we spend our life indulging our hungers and fears then we generate a debt which we are obliged to repay in future lives. Thus we are trapped in the cycle of birth and death. The only way to break this cycle is to stop generating debt. This demands outgrowing hunger and fear. This can only happen when we empathize with the hunger and fear of those around us. When we empathize with the other, and work for them, like Ram, and like Hanuman who serves Ram, we become one with Ram, who has no debts, or desires, and so is eternally tranquil. This union of the self (jiva-atma) with the divine (param-atma) is called moksha. And the easiest way to achieve this is to chant the Hanuman Chalisa a hundred times.

Chaupai 39: Title of the Poem

जो यह पढ़ै
हनुमान चालीसा ।
होय सिद्धि
साखी गौरीसा ॥

Jo yeh padhe
Hanuman Chalisa.
Hoye siddhi
sakhi Gaureesa.

Whoever reads
these forty verses of Hanuman
Will achieve whatever he desires
a claim to which Gauri's lord (Shiva) is witness

This verse contains both the title of the poem, as well as the promise of the poem. Here, for the first time, we learn that this work is called Hanuman Chalisa. And we are being told the benefit of reading it. This is phala-stuti, chanting of benefits. If a Hindu ritual begins with sankalpa, sowing the seed of desire, it always ends with phala-stuti, enumerating the fruits that are promised by the enterprise. And the fruit being guaranteed is the achievement of any desire.

We may want a material desire to be fulfilled, such as the removal of problems, freedom from physical pain, success in an enterprise; or we may want occult help, like powers to control the world; or psychological help, such as contentment and freedom from fear; or we want spiritual success in the form of liberation from the cycle of rebirth. Whatever we desire, this verse guarantees that we will get it when we read the Hanuman Chalisa repeatedly.

What is curious is the word witness (sakshi). It is almost as if the poet is using the traditionally Abrahamic phrase, 'As God is my witness!' The idea of a witness turns the promise into an objective fact, not merely a subjective promise. The witness is

Shiva, the husband of Gauri, who is a guileless hermit, who has no reason to bear false testimony. The chaupai thus amplifies the validity of this composition's promise.

But there is another way to consider this witness. Who is the ultimate witness of the universe? In the Vedas, we come upon the line, 'The bird who watches another bird eating the fruit!' We are the bird eating the fruit, seeking fulfilment of our desires, and the bird watching us eat the fruit is Gauri's lord, Shiva.

Shiva, the hermit form of God, is never hungry, while Vishnu, the householder form of God who manifests as Ram, enables the hungry bird—with the aid of Hanuman—to eat fruit. So while Hanuman enables us to achieve what we desire, the whole act is being watched by the atma within, Shiva, who desires nothing. Perhaps one day, having achieved all that we desire, we will realize how desire never ends, and will see the futility of achievement, and so become witnesses ourselves of the world, and the hunger that motivates people to act and react, die and be reborn.

Chaupai 40: About the Poet

तुलसीदास
सदा हरि चेरा ।
कीजै नाथ
हृदय मँह डेरा ॥

Tulsidas
sada Hari chera.
Keejai Nath
hriday mein dera.

Tulsidas,
God's eternal servant
Yearns that the lord
reside forever in his heart

In this chaupai, we learn that the name behind this composition is Tulsidas. In oral traditions, it was common practice for the poet to insert their name in the composition itself. It was akin to an author signing their name in a written text.

When we study the life of Tulsidas we understand what made him compose the rather simplistic and popular Hanuman Chalisa, after having completed the magnificent and literary Ram-charit-manas.

Tulsidas was born nearly 500 years ago, in the Gangetic plains, and abandoned by his parents at birth because his astrology chart revealed he would herald misfortune. He was named Rambola as the first words he spoke were, 'Ram, Ram!' The nurse who raised him died when he was still a child. When he went looking for his biological parents, he discovered they were already dead. Left to fend for himself, he survived for a long time begging from door to door until, noticing his brilliant command over language, Naraharidas, a disciple of the Ramananda order, took young Rambola under his wing and named him Tulsidas. Tulsidas was educated in Sanskrit and Vedic scriptures as well as the regional language, Awadhi, in Ayodhya and in Varanasi. He heard the story of Ram for the first time from his guru.

In some accounts, Tulsidas did get married. He had a child who died at birth. He was very fond of his wife, and one day, when she decided to stay in her mother's house on the other side of the river, Tulsidas swam across a turbulent river in the middle of the night to meet her. His passion embarrassed her and she yelled, 'If you loved God as much as you loved me, you would have attained moksha!' Thus chastised, Tulsidas left her house. On the way back, he realized that the vine he had held on to, to enter her bedroom, was actually a snake and the log of wood he floated on to get to the other side of the river was actually a corpse. Lust had blinded him. Disgusted, he decided to become a hermit and devoted his life to writing songs about God.

One day, while offering water to a tree, a ghost (preta) appeared before him and offered him a boon for having quenched his thirst. Tulsidas said that he wished to see Ram. So the preta pointed him to Hanuman who was disguised as a leper and had came to Varanasi to hear the narration of the Ramayana. Tulsidas thus saw Hanuman and begged him to show him Ram and Lakshman, and by Hanuman's grace, he saw the brothers riding horses near Chitrakuta, and the next day, Ram appeared before Tulsidas as a boy while Tulsidas was performing his morning ritual of preparing sandal paste. Spellbound by these visions, Tulsidas decided to compose the Ramayana. He first thought of composing it in Sanskrit but Shiva and Shakti appeared in a dream and ordered him to write it in the local language, such that it could be used in a play, and create harmony between the bickering Shaivas and Vaishnavas.

Tulsidas wrote the Ram-charit-manas and it was a huge success. People concluded that Tulsidas was a great saint, for only a saint could write a vernacular work that had the melody of the Sama Veda. Local priests were dismissive of a work not composed in Sanskrit, so to test it they placed it at the bottom of a pile of Sanskrit manuscripts and locked it in the Vishwanath temple of Shiva in Kashi. At dawn, when the bundle of manuscripts was opened, Tulsidas's work was on top with the words 'Satyam, Shivam and Sundaram' on the first page, written by Shiva himself, who had declared the work to be the embodiment of truth, auspiciousness and beauty.

As Tulsidas's work became popular his fame spread far and wide. People said he could even bring the dead back to life by the sound of magnificent poetry. When the Mughal emperor Akbar heard this, he ordered Tulsidas be brought to his court in Agra. Tulsidas was reluctant to travel because he was old, with joint pains and several health problems, including boils on his body. Poverty had taken its toll. However, he was forced to go.

The emperor demanded that the saint show him some miracles. Tulsidas said he was no sorcerer, just a poet and Ram's devotee. Mistaking his honesty for impertinence, Akbar had Tulsidas thrown in jail.

While in jail, Tulsidas composed the Hanuman Chalisa, recollecting how Hanuman had helped Ram, and Sugriv, and Lakshman, and Vibhishan, how he could sort out astrological misalignments, restore physical and mental health, solve the most mundane of problems as well as bestow everything from occult powers to spiritual wisdom to the seeker, while seeking nothing for himself. Suddenly, for apparently no reason, a monkey troop wreaked havoc in the city of Agra and made life miserable in the bazaars, and in the palace. This continued for days, until Akbar let Tulsidas go back to Varanasi, where the poet-saint spent the rest of his life immersed in Ram, and his devoted servant, Hanuman.

Doha 3: Becoming Hanuman

पवनतनय संकट हरन मंगल मूरति रूप ।
राम लखन सीता सहित हृदय बसहु सुर भूप ॥

Pavan tanay sankat harana mangala murati roop
Ram Lakhana Sita sahita hriday basahu soor bhoop

Son of the wind, remover of problems, embodiment of auspiciousness
Along with Ram, Lakshman, Sita dwell in my heart forever

With this doha, ends the Hanuman Chalisa. This is the exit from the mind-temple, where we have invoked, observed, adored, venerated, and petitioned Hanuman, who we describe here in three ways: based on his origin (son of the wind god), based on his function (remover of obstacles) and based on his form (embodiment of auspiciousness). We now invite him to dwell forever in our heart along with Ram, Lakshman and Sita. What do we mean by that? A story explains this well:

Once Hanuman wrote the biography of Ram on a banana leaf. When Valmiki read it, he began to cry, because Hanuman's Ramayana was outstandingly beautiful, of perfect melody and metre, so beautiful that it would overshadow his own work, the Valmiki Ramayana. Feeling sorry for Valmiki, Hanuman tore the banana leaf with his Ramayana on it, and swallowed it whole, thus destroying his Ramayana forever. When Valmiki asked Hanuman why Hanuman had done this, Hanuman replied, 'Valmiki needs Valmiki's Ramayana more than Hanuman needs Hanuman's Ramayana. Valmiki wrote the Ramayana so that the world remembers him; I wrote the Ramayana because I wanted to rediscover Ram. I have achieved my objective. Valmiki needs to achieve his.' Thus, for Hanuman, his work was not about fame and glory, it was yoga: a tool to realize divinity within his heart.

Valmiki bowed to Hanuman for revealing to him the great secret of the Ramayana. It is said that Valmiki therefore took birth again and again, in different times of history, in different geographies, to recompose the Ramayana in different languages, so that he too could re-discover Ram as Hanuman did. Many people see Tulsidas as Valmiki reborn.

The gods are already in our heart and around us. It is upto us to discover them, both without and within. Hanuman Chalisa begins with acknowledging the Hanuman outside. It ends with acknowledging the Hanuman within. What does this mean in practical terms?

To understand this we have to remind ourselves that all living creatures are consumed by hunger and fear. In humans, this hunger and fear is amplified infinitely by imagination. To cope, we use imagination to invent technology and gather resources. But all the resources in the world do not explain the purpose of our life. We remain restless. We either cling to wealth, or use power to dominate others.

In the Puranas, Brahma is blamed for misunderstanding the Vedas and creating a culture that values wealth and power. That is why he is not worshipped. Instead worship is offered to Shiva, the ascetic, who shuns wealth and power, and does not participate in culture.

Shiva beheads the fifth head of Brahma and holds it in his hand for the entire world to see. This fifth head embodies ego (aham), the crumpled mind, which is the offspring of imagined hunger and fear that makes us cling to wealth and seek control over others. Hindus worship Shiva, the destroyer, as he reveals this Vedic wisdom, which the Upanishads call atma-gyan.

Vishnu takes a different approach: he acknowledges and accommodates, even appreciates, the crumpled mind of those around him, and continuously makes available wealth, power and knowledge for them, hoping patiently that they will use their life to outgrow their addiction, and de-crumple their mind. He does not always succeed. But he does not give up. For the world is infinite, and every creature has infinite lifetimes to live, and he has infinite faith in the human potential and infinite patience. Hence, he is the preserver.

In the Ramayana, Brahma is embodied in the ambitious Kaikeyi, in the stubborn Ravana, and in the gossipy public who live in Ayodhya. All three are so self-absorbed that they are oblivious to the consequences of their action on others. Their actions cause the separation of Ram and Sita.

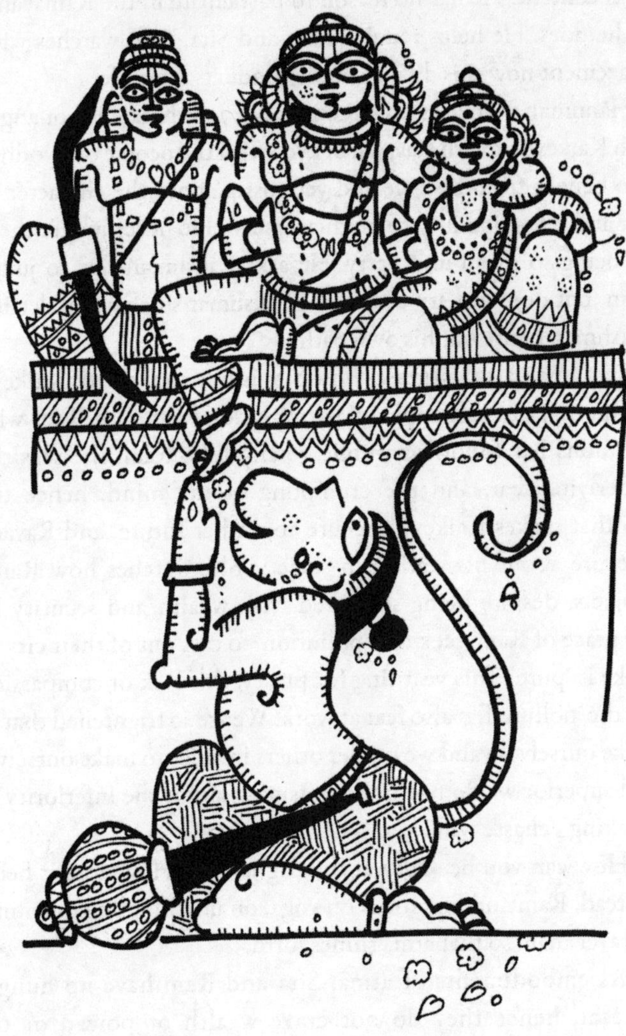

Hanuman is Shiva. The colloquial meaning of his name is the destroyer of the ego. He does not seek wealth, power or knowledge. He is content. He has no reason to participate in the Ramayana, yet he does. He helps reunite Ram and Sita. And watches with amazement how this divine couple conducts their life.

Hanuman witnesses how Ram, unlike Lakshman, is not angry with Kaikeyi, or with Ravana, or even with the people of Ayodhya who benefit from his rule and yet gossip about the character of Sita and her suitability to be their queen. He never judges them for being so mean and petty. He asks Lakshman not to judge them, but does not try to control Lakshman's behaviour, letting Lakshman figure out his own path.

Hanuman also witnesses how Sita is not angry with Kaikeyi, or Ravana, or the people of Ayodhya, or even with Ram who abandons her following public gossip. Like Ram, she sees the underlying fear, and the crumpling of the mind, hence the ego that makes Kaikeyi insecure about her future, and Ravana insecure about his station in society. She watches how Ram's subjects, despite being showered with wealth and security by the grace of Ram, seek out 'pollution' to cast out of their city to make it 'pure'. This yearning for purity, this lack of compassion for the 'polluted', is also fear at work. We are so frightened that to make ourselves valid we render others invalid, to make ourselves feel superior we do not mind gossiping about the inferiority of the king's chaste wife.

How can you be angry at the frightened? How does it help? Instead, Ram and Sita focus on yoga, on uncrumpling the mind, unravel aham so that atma shines forth.

As embodiments of atma, Sita and Ram have no hunger or fear, hence they do not crave wealth or power, or the approval of those around them. They do not seek to control others. They are not dependent like Brahma; they are not independent like Shiva; they choose to be dependable, no matter what the situation.

By repeating the story of Ram again and again, Hanuman understands Ram, and discovers the Ram within him, the ability to be dependable for those who are dependent, even those who are unworthy, like the stream of hungry and frightened devotees who venerate him in his temples.

Likewise, by chanting the Hanuman Chalisa again and again, we hope to understand Hanuman and discover the Hanuman within us.

Further Reading

- Aryan, KC & Aryan, Subhashini. *Hanuman: Art, Mythology and Folklore.* Delhi: Rekha Prakashan, 1994.
- Lutgendorf, Philip. *Hanuman's Tale: The Messages of a Divine Monkey.* New York: Oxford University Press, 2007.
- Nagar, Shantilal. *Hanuman in Art, Culture, Thought and Literature.* Delhi: International Publishing House, 1997.

Acknowledgement

Prof. Purushottam Agarwal, former member of Union Public Service Commission, and former chairman of Centre of Indian Languages, School of Language, Literature and Culture Studies, Jawaharlal Nehru University.

My Gita

By Devdutt Pattanaik

In *My Gita*, acclaimed mythologist Devdutt Pattanaik demystifies the Bhagavad Gita for the contemporary reader. His unique approach—thematic rather than verse by verse makes the ancient treatise eminently accessible, combined as it is with his trademark illustrations and simple diagrams.

In a world that seems spellbound by argument over dialogue, vivaad over samvaad, Devdutt highlights how Krishna nudges Arjuna to understand rather than judge his relationships. This becomes relevant today when we are increasingly indulging and isolating the self (self improvement, self actualization, self realization—even selfies!). We forget that we live in an ecosystem of others, where we can nourish each other with food, love and meaning, even when we fight. So let *My Gita* inform *your* Gita.

'[Devdutt Pattanaik's] subjective and diplomatic craft continues to shine through in his new book. [*My Gita*] marks his transition from mythology to philosophy—one that he makes with deftness and skill.'

—*Scroll.in*

'While [Devdutt's books are] a quick read, the lessons [they] offer are invaluable and will last a long time.'

—*Business Today*

[Devdutt] is a master storyteller, often with delightful new nuances.

—*India Today*

Business Sutra: An Indian Approach to Management

By Devdutt Pattanaik

In this landmark book, bestselling author, leadership coach and mythologist Devdutt Pattanaik shows how, despite its veneer of objectivity, modern management is rooted in Western beliefs and obsessed with accomplishing rigid objectives and increasing shareholder value. By contrast, the Indian way of doing business as apparent in Indian mythology, but no longer seen in practice accommodates subjectivity and diversity, and offers an inclusive, more empathetic way of achieving success. Great value is placed on darshan, that is, on how we see the world and our relationship with Lakshmi, the goddess of wealth. *Business Sutra* uses stories, symbols and rituals drawn from Hindu, Jain and Buddhist mythology to understand a wide variety of business situations that range from running a successful tea stall to nurturing talent in a large multinational corporation. At the heart of the book is a compelling premise: if we believe that wealth needs to be chased, the workplace becomes a ranga-bhoomi, a battleground of investors, regulators, employers, employees, vendors, competitors and customers; if we believe that wealth needs to be attracted, the workplace becomes a ranga-bhoomi, a playground where everyone is happy. Brilliantly argued, original and thoroughly accessible, *Business Sutra* presents a radical and nuanced approach to management, business and leadership in a diverse, fast-changing, and increasingly polarized world.

'Simply brilliant...so different from any other book on business and management.'

—*Asian Age*

'436 pages of pure unadulterated delight.'

—Ravi Subramanian,
Intelligent Entrepreneur

'Pattanaik may have tapped an important emotional need-gap out there, and may have a bestseller on his hands.'

—*Outlook*

'Easy to read, lucid style narrative is very well punctuated with graphics which make the book lively and interactive.'

—*Sunday Standard*